Embracing the Blend

What Mom And Dad Didn't Know They Were Teaching You

Monty C. Ritchings

Monty C. Ritchings
Vancouver, Canada

Library and Archives Canada Cataloguing in Publication

Ritchings, Monty 1951 -
Embracing the Blend: what mom and dad didn't
know they were teaching you / Monty C. Ritchings
Rev. ed.

ISBN 978-0-9781891-3-6

1. Self Actualization (Psychology). I. Title.

BF637.S4R585 2009   158.1   C2009-905566-X

Printed and Bound in Canada
Revised Edition: September 2009

10   9   8   7   6   5   4   3   2

Acknowledgments

My heartfelt thanks go out to all the wonderful people I have encountered throughout my journey in this life. It is through each of you that the wisdom and knowledge contained in this book was revealed to me.

Special thanks, of course, goes to Eva Zanatta for dragging me to the kitchen table back in 2004 and sticking with me while *Embracing The Blend,* was being born.

An Important Notice to Our Readers

My dearest reader, I have written this book with the intention of assisting you by supplying tools and information that I feel are pertinent to the process of revealing you to yourself.

I am a lay counsellor and energetic healing practitioner, long schooled in the art of living. According to those that make up the rules, I am not a therapist. It does not matter to me what label is presented to identify me with others. I support all counseling practices that help individuals heal and empower themselves whether it be in the form of established counseling, energetic healing, yoga, etc. The only thing that matters to me is that you find your own light and express it.

With this in mind, I want to make it perfectly clear that this book is not meant to be a substitute for professional psychological help or any other form of intervention that may be deemed valuable or necessary in your healing journey. This statement is not meant to diminish the value of the information provided in this journal, or to diminish the value of the growth discovered by my clients with my assistance.

It is necessary though, to have you recognize that the lessons procured through working your journey alone are more limiting than through external support.

I strongly urge you, that as you work through the chapters and lessons in this book that you obtain the support of a person capable of supporting you in your self discovery.

This book is intended as a guide for you, not a replacement for the help you may need.

Remember, a candle cannot light itself. My wish for you is that your inner light be illuminated in its own special way so that it adds to the overall light of all mankind.

Namaste

Monty Clayton Ritchings - August 2009

Table of Contents

Introduction

"Embracing The Blend" really conveys the true spirit of the message contained in this book. More often than not, we tend to follow the footsteps of our parents and others whom we have "looked up to" as children without knowingly making decisions about how we really want to live our lives. The choices our forbearers made "worked for them," but did "Mom and Dad" or any of the others ever know there might be more or that things could be any different?

Did Mom and Dad even have the time, or the inkling, to enjoy life's passions, thrills, or perhaps find the opportunity to wander down an unknown road? In front of you now is a choice. Do you want to continue the life created unconsciously by your history, or do you want to learn how to access and embrace the hidden power that waits to be unleashed within you?

The real you that resides behind the walls of your past is just waiting to propel you into your greatest possible, most fulfilling life. You were born into your life for a specific reason. Before you are the tools to understand and complete what you came here to do... in the most wonderful and joyous manner you desire.

The information provided here is not just another regurgitation of the many self-help books already available. Inside are some unique tools, possibly mentioned in other books, but, hopefully presented in a way so you can really make your life work for you.

In your hand is a guide to the unknown roads of your own life. It provides you with the opportunity to travel down streets, avenues, and even the back alleys that you possibly have never chanced to know before. This book is a road map to the most important treasure you can ever own … your "self."

You will now be able to travel into many uncharted aspects of your life, where your deepest passions lie. You may begin to allow the true, complete, powerful you to evolve and express. After all, "Isn't there more to life?"

Finding your own true power by unlocking the doors of your unconscious mind with a key only attainable from within yourself, will give birth to a world you have never before dreamed possible that has always been waiting for you.

The subtitle of this book, *What Mom and Dad Didn't Know They Were Teaching You*, speaks about the internal patterns shaping your current life. From one generation to another, we have continually repeated the same beliefs to no successful conclusion. "Embracing the Blend" helps you stop … and change the continual flow of habitual actions and empower you to make new conscious choices that work best for you.

The point of view of this writing, that is unique, is the focus on eliminating the root causes of what is not working in our lives, rather than burying them under a myriad of affirmations and other positive living tools. We can just quit doing them!

A good analogy of this process is: If you car's gas tank is filled with water, would you put gas into the tank right away or would you drain the water out first, then fill it up?

Clearing your mind of beliefs and habits that do not serve you well is much like the water in the gas tank. The first step in making room for new thoughts and beliefs is to get rid of the "water." In this case, it means disengaging yourself from your past. Then, the magic can really begin!

Within this book, we present a concept that truly revolutionizes that old adage Out with the Old and In with the New!

Once you have completed this book, you will know how to make the changes in your life, so that you can truly live your magic; recognize your passion through "Embracing Your Blend." No longer will you be asking, "Is that all there is?"

It was through my friendship with Eva Zanatta, a true and caring friend, that this book came to be. Our mutual quest for answering the unanswerable questions of life along with her encouragement and much appreciated assistance provided the incentive and energy that eventually resulted in what you hold in your hands today.

Through the many hours of philosophizing about, and analyzing life as we knew it, we realized that throughout our lives till now, we had continually struggled with the bondage of our past habits. We knew innately that claiming our freedom was the most powerful treasure we could ever possess. With this reckoning, we realized that the message needed to be shared with other regular folks like ourselves.

Through my life long journey in studying the workings of the human mind and its relationship to life, I became a core belief counsellor and an intuitive healing facilitator. Although I have studied psychology and sociology and other people-focused modalities, my understanding of what makes us tick developed through the many years of studying human body energy, mysticism and life on the street. Works by great teachers such as Richard Bach, Bruce Lipton, Eckhart Tolle, Louise Hay, Carolyn Myss, John Welwood and Harville Hendrix fed my mind and helped me to see life beyond the norm.

The many clients who have come to work with me over my career are living proof that the process explained herein really works. Their almost spontaneous healing shows that once we realize that however our life seems to be, whether desirable or not, the story originates in our mind and can be changed as quickly as choosing a different outcome requires.

When we come to know that we can change our story anytime we want without struggle, it is then that we know we have arrived at our own true power.

The style chosen for this book is very casual and conversational, sometimes even silly or childlike, just like the many conversations Eva and I have enjoyed over the years. Hopefully, you will realize that even if the tone is not always serious, the message is important and needs to be embraced.

I believe it is easier to learn without having to have a dictionary in hand or a sword to defend yourself with, so I hope you find this journey easy and fun, and that the parts that feel scary disappear easily.

So please get yourself comfortable and join Eva and me as a friend, while we explore the world around us. Let's see what we can do to make life a great place to be.

We both sincerely hope and trust that you will benefit greatly from participating with us.

Love is Not Our First Priority

And then there was the word ... and the word was LOVE. It all started right here a long, long time ago with love, and rightly so! Love is the basis of our existence. Virtually everything we do in our lives is enacted as part of our drive to live in the glory of love. Unfortunately, there is a simple matter that interferes with our utopian concept of living... that dream within each of us that yearns to be fulfilled from the very depths of our souls.

We struggle with it, trying to live with it, sometimes trying to overcome it. No matter what, it is always there. It overshadows the beauty and essence of the love that is rightfully ours. It exists in every cell of our being, until finally; we give up and succumb to it. We call this simple matter...Life.

As a prelude to our conversations, I feel there is something of really great importance that we need to discuss about this matter called life. I can not emphasize the importance of this topic. If you really take the time to understand it, the changes in the way you do your life will be absolutely profound.

We have been taught from time immemorial that love is the basic desire that we search for and crave each day. This statement is true, however, there is something far more important and of greater concern to each of us. Something that drives our lives from a deeper region than even love can access. The desire for it lives in every cell of our body and affects every thought we think … until we finally allow it. That something is:

Safety

Think about it. Which do you think the soldier standing in the middle of a minefield is most concerned about?

Love   or   **Safety**

Which do you think a child watching his parents fighting, is thinking about?

Love   or   **Safety**

As you go about attempting to fulfil the goals you set for yourself and just generally living your life, are you really doing them out of love?

Do you live in your home out of love, or is it because of the feeling of safety you derive from having four walls and a roof around you? Or is it the familiarity?

Do you go to work every day out of the deep love for your job or is it so you can keep yourself safe by keeping food on the table and the bills paid?

Love is important to all of us. We plan our whole life around it. Love is what drives us. We were created through the desire for love.

However, without true personal safety, love has little chance of survival ..... and less likelihood of being expressed in a constructive, meaningful way.

This business about personal safety is serious stuff, so please bear with me. Your patience with acknowledging this information and incorporating it into your life requires that I maintain a serious tone here for a while.

The love I am referring to is not the desire to be with another person, or your pet dog, nor doing your favourite pastime. This love is not the driver of self-made millionaires or the great saviours of the world. The love I refer to is a primordial drive that lets us know that we are alive, the innate feeling within each of us that tells us that we belong to something much bigger than our mortal, egoic individual self. The love that tells us we are okay, that expresses itself in your heart, as joy, just for the sake of living. It is a very simple form of energy, yet we seem to have so much difficulty in finding and keeping it in our lives.

Love is always within reach in our lives, waiting for us to quench our thirst by drinking from its eternal fountain.

Unfortunately, getting through each moment and surviving each day of our lives with all the crazymaking, the boredom and the same old, same old routines keeps us anywhere but in the essence of love.

We all learn to do life based on experience, the experience of survival, existing in a world outside of ourselves.

Every day history repeats itself. . . sometimes quietly and sometimes with the clashing of great brass cymbals, constantly repeating itself, trying to wake us up.

I want you to know and clearly understand:

If you choose to truly know yourself
You must first know true personal safety.

Before you can open yourself to real self-exploration, you need to know you feel safe and comfortable within yourself. As any painful thoughts come forward to release themselves from your unconscious into your present mind, you need to ensure that you do not lose yourself in the thoughts. Letting go of old thought patterns is much like a bubble floating into view and then up, up, and away until it disappears into nothingness. Doesn't that sound better than avoiding and burying those old tapes of long ago? Dissolving them instead of keeping them locked away?

Accepting and allowing your mind to process old thoughts is a safe thing to do, and will help you in untold ways since it is very necessary for your best health, personal growth and overall quality of life. If I could have one wish come true, it would be for every person on planet earth to know and experience true safety. I wish this for you.

Knowing yourself is the greatest asset you can own. It is a tool, which when used properly will never let you down. Once you attain any level of self awareness, it cannot be taken from you. Just by having chosen to participate in our conversation, you will find that you are moved to a new, happier, healthier and more evolved level of consciousness.

Your path may get bumpy at times from the many emotional ups and downs in your life, but if you stick to it and really embrace the process being revealed, you will be rewarded in a way unknowable through any other means. Once it is all over, you will probably wonder why you didn't do it sooner.

Many people who have chosen to not know themselves ask me why I put myself through all this work. Why don't I just grab a beer, flop on the couch and watch TV? It is far easier.

And truly, it is easier ... at least on the surface.

People who choose to know themselves recognize an inner need to change and grow, a feeling of restlessness, and a knowing that life just has to be better than it currently is. Sitting idle, living in a state of numbness is just too painful! And for what?

Living in pain, fear and powerlessness is not truly living!

My belief is that if I am going to hang around this planet for a hundred years or so, this time around, I want to make my life worthwhile to me. I want to make a positive contribution to life as a whole.

It just does not make sense to me that I was born to guzzle beer and die before my TV as my mind melts into mush. Besides, if anyone seriously thinks there is no pain in a life of looking at TV sports through a beer glass, they really need to have a good look at themselves!

In reality, there is more pain afflicted from a hangover caused by too many beers swizzled while watching Monday Night Football than there is in all the effort it will ever require in making your life work for you. So let's set our intention right now...Let's choose to make our journey to personal illumination and happiness as painless and yet enjoyable and profound as possible.

I know I may sound like I am repeating myself but I want to make sure you have got it ...

Unless you develop an appreciation of personal safety and have a reasonable rapport with yourself, you will not fully absorb and master the intention in the lessons herein. Please take the time to understand and integrate what I am telling you before you try to shed the years of misunderstandings and old memories that have shaped your life to this day.

You will miss many opportunities to make really profound changes in your life. Your mind will taint your experience, hold you in your current routine and rob you of the true enlightenment that is your divine right.

Without a strong sense of true safety and comfort with yourself, your subconscious mind may cause your conscious mind to refuse and reject any attempted invasions into those uncomfortable, scary and absolutely sacred beliefs. But please don't panic, your new toolbox is just ahead!

As you progress in your evolution, strong roadblocks may be encountered. Your mind will go around any barriers instead of getting rid of them or passing the safety zone. Your mind wants you to be safe ... according to the way "it" understands safe... The way you always have been "safe." It does not like new thoughts it does not understand or cannot control.

Around any belief, that we choose to hold on to, there is a protective wall that the ego uses to keep the belief and its owner safe. The egoic mind says, "We are not going there."

Monty, could you give me an example of a person "not going there?" Would one be my feeling anxious about public speaking?

It has often been said that the strongest men in the world are not those who lift hundreds of pounds on their backs, but the people who speak in public.

Having to speak in public is a good example of "not going there" if one chooses to stay "safe." After all, there is not a person on earth who does not get an anxious tummy when they have to get up in front of a crowd.

Why? Virtually every one of us developed a belief as a youngster that it was unsafe to speak in front of others or be the centre of attention.

How many times were we told to "be quiet" or to only "speak when spoken to?" How many of us were told that "children are meant to be seen and not heard." Of course, you are not going to go there, Missy. If you were regularly told either of those things, how could you public speak without becoming anxious?

Aren't you the same person who was told to be quiet when you were a child or to be seen and not heard?

You learned the lesson well so getting up to speak in public is very fearful for you. Now as an adult, you act on this belief unconsciously and automatically, as if it is still there activating any time it is required. After all, you are disobeying your parental instructions if you speak up and you would not want to disobey Mom and Dad would you?

That's for sure, I can feel my stomach tighten, my throat gets dry, and my face turns red just thinking about it.

I attribute this to an early childhood event: I came here from Austria when I was six years old. My parents were told to place me immediately into public school. They felt that because I was so young, I would learn English just through regular interaction with kids my same age. However, it really became a problem for me when my grade one teacher made each of us stand up in class and read a sentence on the blackboard.

"Run Spot, Run" might as well have been the Magna Carta for me. I could not even pronounce the words, let alone read them. I had no idea what the words were or meant. I remember going home and asking my mom what a "spot" was. After all, my birth language was Austrian German, not English.

The teacher made me stand there, and repeat the sentence over and over and over. Meanwhile, the other kids would get sore bellies from laughing at my mispronunciations. I felt terribly embarrassed, especially when I found out that "Spot" was the name of a dog. Today I really dislike getting up in front of others. I feel like everyone will laugh at me.

Is this what you mean about "not going there" because of a childhood experience?

Exactly! These kinds of beliefs can always be traced back to childhood. The current belief is: "I cannot public speak."

The wall around you is composed of the numerous automatic thoughts that assist and protect your choice of not speaking in front of "strangers." You are kept "safe" because you chose not to public speak and will as long as this belief has power over you...

The belief is safe because it got validated by your choice to opt out. Each time this happens (You didn't do it.) the "wall" is reinforced making it harder to change the belief.

As you get older and better at not speaking in public, your mind collects and acts out more finding reasons to justify this choice until you don't even "go there" at all.

Depending on how important it is to you to be able to speak in public, you will either make this area of personal growth an issue or you won't. If you choose to become an effective public speaker, you will have to reckon with the related beliefs. I am sure that if speaking out is not in your heart, you will not consider the effort worthwhile. After all, it's not like it is the only issue any one of us has to deal with.

This is an example of what I call a "protective safety mechanism." Like anything that limits any aspect of your life, it doesn't necessarily serve your overall best interest, does it?

I thought safety was positive. By what I am hearing from you, safety is not always in our best interest. What am I not understanding?

This is a critical point. We must learn to recognize and differentiate between true safety and protective safety. True safety is a permanent feature which exists in every person, and is expressed from the deepest part of our self. It is innate and indestructible. All we have to do is know it and embrace it. Hang on and we will learn it.

Protective safety, on the other hand, is instilled through the lessons of our earliest interactions with our environment. Protective safety skills are learned reactions to repetitive external stimuli. Remember all the stuff we kept being told as children?

They come from trying to figure out how to cope with this life. We make mistakes as we try to figure out the rules and we get reactions from the mistakes, from others and ourselves. Touched any hot stoves lately?

The lessons from those experiences teach us how to survive in the life we are developing. They are generally fear based, particularly when they instigate severe repercussions, and annoy bigger people in the process.

These lessons protect us by keeping us where we are right now, hopefully forever in our mind's eye. Our minds learn the routine of living, by repetition. The programs it learns become deeply instilled and will challenge any effort to release their stronghold.

There is little possibility of forward movement in our lives when we are under this power. Your mind is attempting to keep you alive at all costs, with no conscious regard to life in the long-term. Surviving the moment is the only concern. The actions of protective safety are the result of expressing automatic "safety" mechanisms; an unconscious act the mind uses to maintain life in and for the moment. Every day we see classic cases of people trying their level best to cope with life, rather than living life in true safety.

Is protective safety bad?

There is really no such thing as good or bad. Without these coping methods, you might not be alive today. Coping methods, however, are limiting, and that is my biggest concern. As we become aware of how we are living our lives and start to recognize the need to make some changes, we may see that some belief systems (coping methods) work for us and some do not. When we become aware of the ones that are not working for us, we need to be able to recreate them. I am here to help you, to provide you with some tools to achieve this.

How do I recognize when I am using protective safety?

Pay attention to how you are feeling. If you are feeling fear, or just plain feel uncomfortable, or if your mind is completely focused on one particular thought that is causing discomfort, then you are encountering a coping method. Coping methods are a vehicle used to instil and activate protective safety.

How do I recognize when I am feeling fear?

Fear stimulates the Endocrine System in the body. The endocrine system is any of the glands or organs, which produce and transmit chemicals (hormones) that attempt to, maintain homeostasis (balance) in the body. When fear activates this system, it causes the body to tighten the muscles, to speed up nervous reactions, raises the blood pressure and breathing becomes more rapid and shallow.

It feels like your body is closing in on you. Your mind can only focus on the thought that is promoting the feeling of fear. You are now in what is referred to as "fight or flight" syndrome. You are ready to run or fight at the drop of a hat.

Can you give me some examples of the "fight or flight" syndrome?

Flight or fight syndrome is usually activated in extreme cases of fear. However, we need to recognize how we use this action to a lesser degree in every day life situations such as in your previous example of avoiding public speaking or in coping, perhaps, with being in the company of someone you would rather not be with.

Here's a more complicated example I think you can relate to. Let's say you are asked to organize and host a dinner party for 20 people. The stress can be quite overwhelming if it sets off any stressors.

There might be thoughts going off in your head like: "I am not a very good cook. I don't know what to make. How will I entertain all these people?," and "What the heck have I gotten myself into?" etc, etc. Still breathing?

The feeling of knots in your stomach or tightness in your chest muscles will indicate a protective reaction is activated. Recognition is key, as these symptoms are telling you that you feel afraid and that your safety is being challenged.

At this early stage of our learning, let me simply state; that paying attention to these messages is vital.

Is there a difference between protective safety and true personal safety?

Absolutely! True safety is the knowing that you are safe at any time because you are in control (passively), by choice, of your life.

A person who knows their true safety knows instinctively what is required to keep themselves out of harms way. The inner peace they know causes them to attract, at best, no potentially harming events. At worst, because they are conscious of their situation, they can effect damage control. They use common sense.

Truly safe people do not drive recklessly on our streets; they don't hang out at seedy bars or with people who carry weapons or intentionally cause grief for other people.

Truly safe people project positive energy. Since like energies attract, those who express positive energy attract positive people and healthy situations and become "invisible" to undesirable circumstances.

Do I understand correctly then, that protective safety serves us only for the moment but true safety benefits us through our entire life?

Yes, boy you are a fast learner! Think about it, how many people are under- or over-achievers because of the fears they carry?

These people are not able to rest easily inside themselves due to an overwhelming need to feel safe, no matter what the cost. Their inability to feel comfortable within themselves is a limiting belief that drives them to excessive busy-ness which provides an illusion of safety. The mind frick creates a distraction so they don't access what they really fear. We regularly see these kinds of individuals working very long hours, creating massive projects or continually going to school. They just have to keep themselves going to prevent themselves from acknowledging the internal pain of their suppressed feelings that act like a black cloud over their lives promoting the feeling of lack of safety.

Although their lives may be very busy, their efficiency is often quite questionable, as so much of their energy is spent just trying to quell the "noise" in their heads.

Under-achievers do pretty much the same thing except they find themselves in jobs that are not suitable for them. The careers they create do not provide a medium of healthy self-expression. They live within lifestyle limitations such as overly stifling relationships, no relationships or poverty because they hide from themselves in the negative belief of the victim. They feel safe in knowing that "nothing works for them" and thus gives them an excuse not to take actions that would be beneficial for them. Protective safety is their act. It surrounds them in a protective cocoon keeping the dangers of the world far away.

Both of these characters have heads that are filled and overfilled continuously with thoughts that "jam the signal" that is trying to tell them that something is not okay, and that they need to do something about it. However, a belief that keeps telling them that if they keep their minds busy and distracted, they "don't have to go there" as we described earlier. Eventually, they will pay the cost in illness and financial difficulties.

Is this true of all people who are over or under achievers?
Should everyone strive for mediocrity?

Again, it is not a case of better or worse. It is a case of recognizing how we "do" our lives, living in our choices. Protective safety methods are designed so that there is little or no potential for running into belief systems that have been guarded away in protective vaults in the deep recesses of the mind or that can cause any kind of perceived emotional pain. As life occurs, the expended energy bounces off any of this "protective safety," much like playing air hockey or pinball. If one continually lives inside their safety (coping) mechanisms, they cannot really come to know healthy safety. They never get to their true nature. They can only know the life that expresses as a result of their beliefs. They become, in effect, the persona of the beliefs.

A person who knows true safety can be a very busy and productive person. They live life according to their own drives, within a healthy set of boundaries. Their lives are filled with abundant opportunities that propel them further into knowing and expressing the creative giant within them, in every aspect of their lives. A person with good personal safety creates their own best possible careers, attracts healthy people and relationships into their lives and enjoys being who they are. They live life naturally with little effort and at a flow that is natural for them. They live life in balance. They deal with the trials of life as an opportunity to know themselves more intimately and do not blame others for their perils.

If one does not know what they do to maintain safety, or how they keep themselves safe and protected, how can they possibly risk opening up to explore their inner world?

Good point. The very mechanics we use for our own self-preservation also prevent, or at least inhibit, access to the magic within us.

We have learned to protect ourselves automatically and learned it well. We have learned to over-magnify our fears, and thus let fear become our master. When man (and all animals for that matter) was created, fear was imparted upon us to act as a guide, not to be our captor. In so much of our lives, we have lost sight of the light that shines within us because darkness has been allowed to overshadow the beauty that is our truth and strength. Learning to recognize the physical symptoms of fear is a good starting point.

The question that begs to be answered at this moment is: How do we know when we are controlled by fear?

This is an essential component of recognizing how we maintain safety. Most of us, if not all, have learned that this world can be a very scary place. As a result, we have unconsciously created instinctual behaviours that automatically pull us inside ourselves, taking us away from our power to respond consciously and robbing us of our greatest potential. The trade off is that we "believe" we are safe. Talk about protective safety!!

As I stated before, when we feel threatened, we need to learn to be adept at recognizing the physical symptoms of fear. Our bodies feel tighter, our breathing becomes shallower, and our heart beats faster. We tend to get caught up in the activities of our minds as we become focused on, even obsessed by our thoughts. If the fear is great enough, we pull away from other people, possibly becoming very quiet or alternatively very loud as we lash out at the world--- all in the name of safety.

Some people drive too fast, talk too much or too loud, commit crimes, join gangs or become pregnant, all out of fear. I cannot tell you often enough:

Awareness is the key!

As we become more aware of how we get through life, we realize the repetitive actions that we would rather not be doing. Yet, for some unknown reason, we just can't seem to get past them. The person who can't seem to public speak is a perfect example. What real danger is there really (as referred to earlier) in getting up and saying something in front of others? Another example would be a person who compulsively eats. They often do not even realize there is food going into their mouths because it has become such an automatic reaction.

I think I am beginning to understand, but what is your point?

My point is, and what I would like to offer you at this moment, is a choice. A choice to remain stuck in beliefs that keep you in "protective" safety or take a chance and learn to embrace and live your life in "true" safety.

During our time together, you will learn more about yourself, your life and safe keeping methods that are good for you for the long-term. You will learn how to develop healthy coping methods and let go of counter-productive ones. Keep the good safety, let go of the protective safety,

The result being more and higher energy for those parts of your life you enjoy and strive for along with a lot more peacefulness, happiness and love.

How do we begin?

Let's begin by seeing if we can develop some safe learning conditions. This way, when we get to the challenging parts, we can proceed more easily because we know we are okay, and that we will make it to the other end, and long past.

There are some things I would like you to know before we start:

- You do not have to change anything about yourself.

- You may progress as slowly or quickly as you choose.

- You are a free expression of life exactly as you are.

- You have free choice. Nobody can force you to live any other way than how you choose.

- There are no requirements for you to be anything other than who you are right now.

If changes are warranted:

- You must be the one who decides that they are right for you.

- Should you become aware of an aspect of yourself that may cause you concern, it is up to you to decide whether it needs to be changed or not. The part that you know without question is the real you.

I am offering you right now, some awareness and some tools that will support you in your choices to express yourself as you please.

I am really glad to hear that! I know that I learn best when I can rely on my own instincts and feelings rather than having to adopt someone else's beliefs in order to feel okay with myself or to get a better handle on the world. Where do we start?

When I began my journey into the study of the human psyche, I learned at an early stage that the common perception of self is somewhat distorted. If you ask the average person who they are, they will likely reply: "I am a carpenter, I am a father, I am a skier" or "I am this body that you see before you," or a host of another million answers.

None of these answers is correct, for if you remove these images or change them, the person is still there. Therefore, we are not our bodies, our minds, our egos, our thoughts or our emotions. This is critical information for any person who wants to impart serious change in their lives.

So who am I then, if I am not any of these things?

The "true" you is that part of you that resides deep inside your being, that part of you that you cannot see, but you know is there. You can sense it. It is the part of you that lights up when you smile the part of you that knows without having to think that recognizes goodness, beauty and love.

Does fear stop us from being in this part of ourselves?

When fear strikes, it resonates in your mind and body through your ego. It serves great purpose when it speaks. It wants to keep you safe. However, when fear is engaged, if it is powerful enough and if you are not consciously in control of your mind's activities, it can inhibit your ability to really be safe. It limits your consciousness to those thoughts that are currently provoking the feeling of fear and the related protective safety mechanisms, preventing us from making alternative and hopefully, healthier choices. Try it for yourself the next time you feel yourself in fear mode. Try to think about something else. Until you become used to diffusing these automatic mechanisms, they will rule your life.

Why was fear created?

If you can learn to recognize fear as a feeling, a tool for protecting yourself, then you have taken a large step in understanding how to maintain your safety in a beneficial manner. Fear is the ultimate safety device. Using it properly will enhance your life.

Learn how to recognize fear and be okay with the feeling. When you feel it, step back and ask yourself," What do I need to pay attention to?"

If you can do that and heed the warning, you will be safe. More importantly, you have taken an important step in taking control of your life.

Fear is just a tool. You are not the fear. Fear was created as an expression of your emotional body to relay information pertinent for keeping you alive, evolving and most importantly- safe.

Is there a relationship between fear and anger?

A counsellor whom I worked with years ago told me something that I consider to be probably the most profound statement I have ever heard in regard to my own personal growth.

"Anger is a socially acceptable way of showing fear."

When I understood what she meant, I knew my need for anger had lost its power. I knew that when I felt anger, I needed to find out where the fear was. This was a giant step in developing safety for me. Thanks Wendy.

Once she had told me that, I realized that when I felt anger, I really was feeling fear. Anger had been one of my major issues, one that I just seemed unable to change......at least until that moment. I knew then that if I felt anger, I really was feeling fear. If I felt fear I was feeling unsafe. I then did not need to do anything about my anger, I only needed to determine why I did not feel safe … and do something about it.

Wow, that's a lot of information! Let's break it into point form, so I can make sure I understand. Safety can be attained by recognizing that:

- *I am not the emotions I feel*

- *The emotions I feel are a separate entity from me*

- *My personal safety is not dependent on being the emotions I currently feel*

- *I am not those nasty thoughts in my head*

- *My personal safety is not dependent upon acting out or reacting to what those thoughts are telling me*

- *I exist now and will continue to live long past this moment of fear without having to accept the beliefs in the thoughts in my head*

- *Whether I accept the "truth" of these thoughts or not has no bearing on my future or my safety unless I choose to give them the power. I am more powerful than my thoughts ... always!*

- *I am safe just by the realization that I know that I am safe.*

How did I do? Am I correct in my understanding that all I need to do to feel safe right now is to recognize and see myself separate from my feeling of fear?

You are amazing, girl! Yes, the first step is just recognizing that you are not your emotions, and that includes your fears. Fear is an essential tool for survival. Keep it that way. It is not meant to run or ruin your life. Give recognition to what is promoting the feeling of fear, but do not become the fear. Fear is meant to keep you safe. Know you are naturally safe and fear becomes a tool.

One more thing. Can you expand on fear as a tool? The very mention of the word still leaves me feeling afraid and unsafe. It seems you see fear as a positive. I feel a bit confused.

Wouldn't you like to have an early warning system that serves only to keep you safe when you are encountering an old belief system that may not be serving you well?

Fear is a tool that provides this service. It's like the traffic light at an intersection.

Green indicates no fear. Go ahead.

Yellow means proceed with caution. There are concerns to be aware of.

Red means STOP, LOOK and LISTEN right now. You may be in danger, there is information you need to know.

If you can listen to the message fear is trying to tell you, and respond to the information rather than the feeling, your need for protective safety will be reduced and you will be much safer than any other method can provide. Fear, when used as a tool, is very positive. It is a component of true safety.

I think I am getting the drift now. Just to make sure, can you explain personal safety in a different way? I really want to make sure I understand.

Sure. The issue of safety cannot be undervalued. How we maintain our safety is key to how fully we express ourselves. Understanding our relationship to safety is paramount to moving forward in our lives.

In the world of meditation, there is a term which expresses the true feeling and intention of what I am calling true safety—be an "empty vessel," a structure that is solid and complete unto itself whose identity is not contingent on what is in it.

Can you imagine yourself as an empty jar? Just for your mind's sake, let's be an earthen jar shaped like an old milk bottle, wide at the base narrow just below the top and wide at the rim, with a big hole for letting fluids into our being from sources far above us.

Take some deep breaths.

Let yourself relax.

Let go of all your thoughts.

As you release, begin to feel yourself relaxing into your natural body composure.

Although you are solid like the milk jug, you have become an empty vessel. We are always an empty vessel. It is our natural state. When we get caught up in our thoughts, the vessel gets filled, often to overflowing. We lose, albeit temporarily, sight of our true selves and become the contents.

When we see ourselves as an empty vessel, and we have accepted that we are not our thoughts or feelings, we can watch our jar fill and empty as we move through life. Thoughts come and go. Feelings come and go. By realizing that we are not our thoughts or feelings, we have no attachment to them and freely release them knowing that our safety or our identity are not in jeopardy.

It also allows us to enjoy the thoughts or feelings more easily as they occur, because we are not at risk.

They are only for our learning and our amusement.

Everyone has this empty vessel within. Access to it only requires recognition. Separating oneself from the "contents" automatically places us in safety and in the empty vessel. After all, does the milk bottle ever become the milk?

By taking the time to STOP and be the empty vessel, you break the flow of continual activity in you mind. If the activity is not fed by continual attention, it will eventually stop.

Life will continue to have its more "interesting" moments. At time, we will still find ourselves filled with anger, grief, love, happiness and any other emotions. We will express those feelings and emotions but, since we are not identified with them or attached to them, they will have no power over us. They will flow through like water pouring down a drain.

Treating our feelings and emotions in this manner makes having these "life connections" much more fun. Even fear and anger can be enjoyed if we know we don't have to be consumed by them or react to their demands.

Is that what you refer to as "detachment?"

You're getting good at this. A sense of detachment allows us to enjoy feelings and express them, while recognizing that we are not them. They are just things we do. They colour our life.

Is detachment different from disassociation?

Yes, good point. It is important to differentiate between detachment and disassociation. In disassociation, the person denies having the feeling and therefore holds the energy of the feeling in their body. This is a coping method, a potentially dangerous one, as you will read later. Being a "tough guy" is typical of a person who is disassociated from their feelings. A person who has disassociated is still attached to their feelings, even though they are denying it. Nice trick, but no jellybeans.

When we do not separate ourselves from our thoughts and feelings, we use coping methods in order to maintain safety. If we are not separated from them, then we are attached. We cannot be conscious of our empty vessel.

When we are filled with these kinds of attachments, we will either perceive a distorted view of the world or we will not be able to accept new information.

Is disassociation ever a useful tool?

Don't get me wrong. Disassociation is an important and powerful tool for coping with certain situations. However, it should not be used as a method for getting through life on a regular basis. Certain jobs and situations require disassociation in order for the person to perform. Could you imagine an ambulance attendant or a police officer who is attending to a motor vehicle accident trying to do their job if they allowed their emotions to interplay?

Disassociation allows the mind to stay focused on the scenario at hand with little or no outside information penetrating. Good short-term strategy. After the situation is completed, it is important for the person to return to openness. Many high-stress occupations include a "debriefing" once the event is concluded.

These attachments inhibit the ability to see clearly. One cannot truly know peace or joy and cannot clearly receive information that may be vital to their own best interest.

Detachment is a long-term proposition. Really enjoying and embracing our lives means truly feeling life coursing through our veins. It allows us access to our true power and to express our individual creativity.

People who are empty vessels are more relaxed. They smile easily and are healthier. Life is more peaceful because they do not attract drama in order to feel alive. They are more able to receive the fruits of life because they have room and a willingness to receive.

They have no need for walls to protect them, as they know deep inside they are safe and protected, just by the fact that they are. They also have no need for the adrenaline rush that comes from putting themselves into danger.

෴

I like the concept of the empty vessel, but you know me, I need lots of examples. I can understand separating my consciousness from my feelings and thoughts but seeing myself as a jar is a bit of a stretch. Could you provide another analogy that is easier for me to understand?

It is definitely one of the great challenges of spoken language. I use my words according to my concept of what I understand and you try to understand them according to yours. I am not sure how we ever get anything across. Patience is definitely a virtue, that's all I have to say. Let's look at this from another view.

A phrase that is bandied about these days amongst the New-Agers is "witness consciousness." Let me explain this and see if this will help.

Going back to the discussion about who we are, it was stated that we are not our minds, our bodies, our egos, our emotions, or our thoughts. Following on this premise, let's imagine that you are sitting in a movie theatre. Your "stuff" (thoughts, feelings, etc) is on the movie screen. As you sit there, you realize that you are separate from them. You can see yourself as a separate entity from them. You are "witnessing" them. They are on the screen doing whatever they are doing; you are in the chair watching. You cannot be in two places at one time, so therefore they cannot be you, nor you them.

You, in this scenario are the empty vessel. The stuff on the movie screen is merely entertainment, that which fills your jar.

Gandhi was once heard to say that he had so much to do on this particular day, that he was going to have to meditate for two hours rather than his usual one because he had so much to do. It would be nice to have the time to sit quietly for two hours per day. I am sure if we did, we would be inspired to be as great as our beloved Gandhi.

For now, if you can just stop for a few seconds whenever you get wound up, so you can break the energy flow of the thoughts and fears that are hounding you, you will move dramatically closer to true safety.

How would that relate to real life?

Let's go back to the dinner party scenario. You have twelve people coming over for dinner tonight. You like to really strut your stuff when you entertain, so you are motivated. Right? Sound good?

Yeah, Sure I can feel the pressure already. Couldn't we just order in?

Can you see how you are already in fear mode, just with the idea?

Yes, my mind is already racing.

Tell me what thoughts are going off in your head.

I feel like I don't have enough time. I am not sure what I have at home already to cook or what I need to buy. I didn't clean the oven. There is a sink full of dishes. What are you going to be doing while I am cooking? Why can't you help me?

What am I going to wear? Oh, gosh, my mind is just racing.

Where are "you" in this moment?

Caught up in my thoughts.

Now, take a deep breath and allow yourself to relax. Feel your body. Let yourself sink into the chair. Relax for a few minutes. Now look at the thoughts going on in your mind as if they are on a movie screen. What happens now?

I feel more relaxed. My mind is less busy. I can feel the intensity of the situation mellowing. I know that you are going to do all the cooking instead, while I have a nice leisurely bubble bath. Gee, I like this process.

I think I liked this better before you learned to separate yourself from your thoughts. Maybe ordering in sounds good after all!

The bottom line in understanding all this business about safety is this. If you can bring yourself to a point where you can be truly comfortable and relaxed with yourself, and I emphasize the word "truly," so that you can be in present time with no coping mechanisms going off, you are in true safety.

The only time frame in which you can make changes to your life or make any decisions in is present time. Past and future can only influence the thoughts of present time, and only if you let them.

It is important that we learn to live consciously in present time using the past as a resource and the future as a "carrot."

If you want to be a marathon bicycle racer, do you have to re-learn how to ride your bike every time you get on it? Does having a related goal that is worthwhile to you energize you to keep going, no matter what?

The same is true if you wish to change a past trauma. If you recognize the trauma as a past learning experience (by leaving out the old attached emotions) and choose a different outcome you will eventually permanently change the belief that forms the basis of the remembrance.

If you can learn to use this condition of living in present time as the anchor for your life as often as you can, you will live a far more functional, successful life. If you can learn to make your decisions from this space, rather than from an emotionally gyrated level, you will make better decisions for yourself. Emotions are only supposed to juice up your life, they are not meant to run it.

Later on, we will discuss more about safety. We will also give you some more really neat tools for promoting and developing a strong sense of safety within yourself.

Try practicing these tools for a few minutes each day.

For now, we are at least at a point where we can hopefully begin to explore the activities within our minds without feeling that our survival is impacted in any way by touching on the thoughts we encounter.

Take a deep breath and relax! You have earned it!

The Blend

Here is an interesting bit of philosophy for you to ponder.

Nothing can exist without a history.
Nothing new can be created from nothing.

Our starting point in each day is the end of our history from the day before, every little piece of it. Our automatic responses re-activate daily, as we open our eyes to begin the new day, and, hopefully, they go to sleep as we close our eyes to sleep. It never stops.

But from where do the automatic responses originate? They had to have come from somewhere. If they were hard wired in, wouldn't they be the same for everyone? But they are not the same, not even amongst family members.

They come from … Our own personal history.

We have learned to live our lives in the way we do through the repetition of what has worked for us in the past. And since it worked for us before, what makes us think it won't work for us today? Or tomorrow for that matter?

If nothing else, at the very least, it gets us through the day so we then can go to sleep once more, and hopefully create yet another day tomorrow.

So, what is our history?

How did it come to be?

What caused our history to be what we believe it is?

There are two parts to the answer of what created our past. The first is the result of the communion of our parents, the act of physically creating us. This gave us our body. The second, the part we are concerned about here, was created through our interactions with life and our environment, the learned experiences, since the day of our conception.

Both of these parts are aspects of your "Blend," the energies that make up "you." At this time we are only going to discuss the second, the interactions, how we all learned about living life.

When you were conceived (without including any discussion about past lives), the chalkboard of your mind was blank. No pre-existing knowledge was present for you. There was no history for you to rely upon.

WHAM!! The moment of conception arrived and your life has begun! As you grew inside your mom, you received her impressions about life. Like all parts of her body, whatever went on (or off) in her mind affected you. Her moods, stress levels and her joys all helped to pave the way.

This is the development of cellular memory which begins at the moment when the egg and the sperm met- creating you. Your "Blend" has begun. Welcome to the world!

The blend is the combination of everything, but in particular the genetic, family and cellular memories that molds and shapes your life on every level of your existence.

The blend that expresses as your personality is based on how you "emotionally and unconsciously perceive the world" as it evolves in every second of your life, molding it as you make choices that define and promote your understanding of your world.

Simply, you are the culmination or blend of everything that has happened in your past. This is a continuous evolution until the day you pass the finish line.

So, let's follow the process of the evolution that is you ... and me ...us ...and everyone else. Let's see if we can determine how we got where we believe we are. The major consolation in understanding this perception, as we will learn and appreciate over this journey, is that everything is changeable.

Most of our impressions of the world pre-birth develop directly through being part of Mommy's body and thus a recipient of her thought patterns. If Mommy is happy, especially about being pregnant, then life is good. If Mommy is having a bad day, then things may be not so good. But that's okay, because as you get bigger and get hands and feet, you can let Mommy know when you are not in tune with her choices.

Everything Mommy does makes an impression on you while inside. What Mommy eats, drinks and smokes??? affects her body and yours. When Mommy works, exercises or makes love, it all affects you ... All of it scoring points, in your emotional development and makeup.

This is very evident when doctors and other professionals talk about problems that babies have to deal with such as fetal alcohol syndrome, drug addiction, etc. Unfortunately, those statistics don't chalk up any numbers about the kids that receive tons of love and affection from a mom that is happy and mature.

ᕙᕗ

And what about Dad?

He is important too, but to a lesser degree at this time, as baby is not physically a part of his body. How Dad treats Mom during pregnancy, how Dad accepts becoming a father and how Dad "plays" with baby before birth has a direct affect on baby's disposition. All of these actions assist in creating the basis of all development.

Dad's habits also have an affect on the unborn child, but more so prior to conception. If Dad is an alcoholic or a drug user, his sperm will carry the evidence to his unborn child. However, Dad, the athlete and upstanding caring citizen also gets to the child's memory base.

Babies do not have the capacity to think consciously or individually pre-birth. Thinking for baby is a result of a process that releases chemicals in Mom's body through her endocrine system (we'll check that out later too!) that cause a reaction in baby's body. (Baby is actually an organ within Mom during pregnancy just like her liver or kidney, etc) This is the beginning of how everyone learns to develop an affinity with the world they are coming to know.

Many parents today are realizing that talking to the unborn child, playing music for baby, taking the time to revel in the joy of the creation forming in Mom's tummy and embracing the beauty of the love shared between Mom and Dad are critical to baby's well-being. There is nothing like a good start!

It is my belief that the soul enters the baby's body with the first breath, at the time of birth. Once separation from Mom's body and mind is completed, thinking as a separate individual began. Prior to birth, you have already learned that you need to have your needs met. You eat, sleep, remove waste and other simple functions automatically while inside Mom.

Once baby arrives in the outer world, the automatic caring process is ended forever. This is an important concept that seems to have been largely forgotten in today's world and is the basis for many life and relationship challenges.

Independent life in this world has begun. With no rules except what you have learned in the womb, you must find a way on your own to have your needs met. Also, just to add to this challenge, the ability to language has yet to be learned, so you have another obstacle in getting what you want.

You will learn to have your needs met by developing ways to communicate with your environment. This environment may include Mom, Dad, brother, sister, cat, dog and an array of other possible participants. You learn to smile when you like something or someone, push away other things (especially food like strained broccoli), coo, and of course cry (the long-standing favourite). You respond and learn from this scenario…and very rapidly, at that, if Mom and Dad are mature enough to realize that your needs must come before their own, for now. As well, your big brother and sister will dote over their new sibling. Even the cat will act appropriately. You are heading for a life of absolute perfection.

But hold on! What's this? Mom and Dad are talking very loud today? Big brother has his druthers too, because he doesn't want beans for dinner again. To add to the milieu, sister is feeling neglected and is also demanding attention. Even the cat is feeling frustrated and wants to be left alone.

All of a sudden, the real world is setting in! And so is your own personal flavour of the blend.

We don't usually assume that babies think (at least not about who's going to win American Idol or the concepts of Plato), however, an unconscious type of thinking does occur right from conception.

As a baby you were faced with all kinds of decisions, often about questions that may never be completely answered in your whole life. You developed an understanding regarding life in general, how to survive, how to have your needs met. Through all of this, you developed your "blend." You learned what love means and looks like through your own eyes. You learned how to keep yourself safe. You started to learn about your own likes and dislikes.

In a perfect family, the child will incorporate a view of life that is warm and cuddly, fun, safe to explore, with all the food he can eat, clean diapers and more attention than he could possibly ask for.

However, reality sets in again. Mom needs to look after the other kids; after all, they have needs too! But your diaper is wet... and you are teething as well. You scream (in baby talk) "Yo Mama! Fix me up! I am not happy! I don't like this!"

To no avail! Mom is caught up in other things for a few moments. Unfortunately, a few moments to Mom are eons to a baby. You are now upset! "Hey, my needs are not being met! I am not feeling loved!"

The beginning of dissension is now setting in. This perfect world is flawed! So what to do? During this time, you are developing survival skills, created through your perceptions and from your level of understanding.

You will try other methods to have your needs met. Some will work and some will not. Some will be met with love and approval. Some will be met with blatant disapproval (and possibly a smack on the rump ... or worse). As situations repeat, you start to get the hang of the program.

You learn that grandma likes to feed you and bring you toys. Grandpa calls you "his prince or princess" and lets you chew on his finger. Mom is the one who comes running at night when you holler. Dad likes to feed you too, but gets food all over and down your front. Sister only likes to play with you if she can dress you up in outfits that are simply not within the range of your well-developed sense of colour and fashion. The cat? Well it has sharp claws that really hurt.

As you grow and become a toddler new adventures begin, as your world expands. You start to socialize, share and communicate with words. New people include other children and more grown-ups. You learn new lessons by interacting with these new people, all helping to "create" your blend.

Babies live in a "me first and only" world. When numerous little ones congregate, the war erupts, as each of them tries to maintain their own "me first" position.

High-level training begins as baby finds out that others have needs and big people have rules. Socialization can be very hard on the ego. Expectations and demands are added to Junior's learning curve. Having all his needs met instantaneously is now a distant memory.

For you? It's potty training, walking, feeding yourself and a host of other jobs. The "Blend" has now moved to a new level.

As more and more people and situations participate in your life, the blend shapes the personality. Every child's personality is unique because their blend is different from anyone else's. No two people can have identical blends.

Generally, according to psychologists, personalities are about 90% shaped by the time a person is around seven years old.

The final opportunity to mould the basic beliefs of your blend begins around age five. School, teachers and other "non-resident" authority figures move in.

At the time of entering the school system, you are still very impressionable and vulnerable. You are now forced to spend a "millennia" away from home and the safety of Mom. Some other woman places demands of unfair proportions on your time, and reprimands you for being independent of thought. Love is a very low priority in this equation. The teacher is a nice person (who can't hug you for fear of being charged with sexual abuse) but has 33 kids to control, while hopefully creating a good, safe learning environment.

Adult type learning now begins. You learn new things like arithmetic and spelling. You also improve your skills in getting approval, sharing, manipulating, fighting and competitiveness and about living in structure.

As life progresses, many other factors occur very commonly that influence your blend. They fit into two categories: interactions with other people and environmental issues. Every minute of your life is filled with opportunities for creating more depth to the blend. Every time you interact in life, it either creates a new belief or it strengthens an existing one. As you age, the likelihood of creating new beliefs decreases, but existing beliefs can and will be strengthened due to circumstances that trigger similar feelings.

It would be idyllic to believe that you would only develop belief systems that are the best possible for you. However, life goes on. Remember your situation with the teacher that helped shape your fear of public speaking? I am sure the teacher had good intentions but look at the result. So much for your life as a famous news broadcaster!

Since we, as adults have likely not worked through all of our quirks, the likelihood of our children developing some challenges is reasonable. Even if we have developed a life style of complete perfection, we still cannot control their take on life or the influences of other people on them.

The best we can do is provide children with a good solid base to work from. We need to take the time to focus on what we feel will implant the best possible information into their minds. Being mindful, of purposely programming them is the best defense rather than the haphazard learning that usually occurs.

Oftentimes, situational problems influence the blend negatively. At the time they occur, they manifest due to a differing set of needs between family members. "Latch-key" kids are a good example. Young children are left to fend for themselves because Mom and Dad need to both work in order to afford an acceptable life style.

They believe they are doing what is best for the family. However, Junior sees it as not having his needs met. He needs attention; help with his homework and guidance in setting boundaries. Since Mom and Dad are not there to satisfy these needs, he develops beliefs that will likely be problematic in the future.

In many societies where there are strong family structures, this problem occurs far less often. Mom and Dad work full time, but Grandma and Grandpa live with them and take on the role of molding the minds of the children. Children actually develop a much broader view of the world and develop stronger family ties and values when they regularly experience family through multiple generations. Issues about abandonment are less likely to develop since there is always someone around.

The cost of getting by has a huge effect on children. It impacts them in so many different ways in each family unit. Whether it is latch-key kids, a single parent family, or perhaps the parents just plain do not earn enough money to get by on, the insecurity in the family situation will promote insecurity in the child unless there is conscious influence by the parents that creates a more secure and safe environment.

Environmental influences play a large part in developing the child's view of life as well. A child who grows up in the country will have a completely different perspective than a child who grows up in the city. Although children can certainly get into trouble anywhere, the effects of the geographical location will influence their life. Many kids who live in the city spend their lives watching television or playing computer games while the country child will be off doing chores, learning about animals, plants and nature in general. Neither situation is necessarily any better than the other, but their surroundings will impact their blend.

Another major environmental concern is the social situation occurring outside the home. Regions that are war torn or ravaged with disease or extreme poverty will have a distinctly different effect than the more preferable areas where all is serene, healthy and safe.

No matter what the external influences are in our life, we will develop beliefs as life goes on. This is an automatic function. Understanding how the beliefs are created and how they influence our lives and how we can manage them is paramount in the process of our evolution.

By age seven, the blend is largely complete. The average child has interacted with hundreds of people of various sizes and persuasions. The interaction with all these people has created another unique person.

Can you understand now, how much your childhood played in the shaping of your life today? Just wait, there's lots more to come yet.

You Are Always Who You Believe You Are!

Computers are amazing gadgets! Put the right information into them and they can produce wonders: draw pictures, search the Internet, do math, store data! It will do virtually anything you want …if you have the right information with the right software programs.

There is a term in the computer world called …GIGO … Garbage In, Garbage Out. This simply means that what you put into the computer determines what you get from it.

Computers also require good user knowledge in order to garner the best possible benefit from it. Have you ever tried opening an MSExcel document in MSWord? Looks pretty funny doesn't it? And not very functional!

Like everything else that man has ever invented, the computer was originally created by Mother Nature. Our original computer is the human brain; only our brain is hundreds of times more capable than even the most powerful computer today.

Our brain needs to be operated much like a computer in order to use it most effectively. It is really too bad that no one has invented a simple user guide for it. It would give us much better functionality if we really understood our brain's workings and capabilities, and the inherent dangers of inputting inappropriate information.

We have a great operating system (our minds) that is installed at birth. However, the user, at the time of recording the secondary levels of operation (belief systems), has little comprehension of the impact the "software" they are programming will have on the balance of their lives. How much of the information we input into our minds is "Excel" information being run in "Word?"

Without coming to a clear understanding of what we have done to ourselves through these unconscious choices, we cannot really come to know and embrace our full potential, or, for that matter, live a truly happy and satisfying life.

Apparently, we use as little as 10% of our potential brainpower. Isn't it such a shame that so much goes to waste?

I believe that much of that waste of brain power is caused by **Core Beliefs** and that is what we are going to chat about today.

I know that looking back at my childhood; I can sure see the relationship between my poor grades in school and the amount of emotional turmoil that was going on. Life wasn't much fun back then!

If we could access the untapped part of our brain, and then use it to accelerate our life capacity, wouldn't we be even more amazing than we presently are? And a whole lot more liberated? How come we don't seem to be able to get at this part of our mind?

My goal for you and for me is to see if we can get even close to this by the time we are finished. I think that if we can manage our beliefs better, we will be able to use more of our gray matter. Worth a try?

As I have stated before, at the time of conception, the human mind is a clean slate as far as having knowledge of how to function on this life plane. However, as the child develops inside his mother, his mind is subjected to its first impressions of the world through Mom's message centres. After birth, the child learns by interacting directly with his own world. Through this process, he makes "unconscious" decisions about life, based on how he has come to understand the rules that have affected his life to that point (which likely aren't that many but that is all he has to go on).

Psychologists claim that children develop about 90 per cent of their personality by the time they are about seven years old. The personality forms largely through their interactions with their environment. They form belief patterns based on what they "learn" through these interactions, and then express them through the personality. The more often a given set of circumstances repeat, the more prevalent the belief system will be seen in the personality. (The personality must be separated by definition, from the character of a person. The personality is an expression of the temporary "self," which exists only in this lifetime, whereas the character is part of the soul, or inner self, which is infinite. When a person dies, so does his ego and personality.)

This is a fundamental rule of life, so please listen again...

We all learn our beliefs and we all learn them exactly the same way... by experience. The more often we experience a particular type of stimulus or a particular situation, the more likely we are to develop a belief relating to it.

To put this in plain English, the more times something happens to us, or the more times we are told something, the more likely we are to believe it. (Just like the computer, it memorizes a function; hit the right button and the same action will always occur.)

When children become adults, they usually rely on the same old belief systems that they developed when they were little. (Likely, because no one told them they could be changed or that they even had them!)

Our current focus then is the exploration of the early belief systems of childhood, how they developed and how they affect a person who is trying to cope with life as an adult (After all isn't an adult just an older model of his younger child?).

Much like computer software, it is very possible to re-program our minds to work better for us.

The "software" programs we develop for getting through life are commonly known as Core Beliefs. They are called such because they form the very essence or core, of the understanding that forms as the operating system of our lives. They are the basis of how we "see" life.

Every decision and action we make throughout our lives is filtered through, and affected by our core beliefs.

For the purpose of this conversation, we will refer to Core Beliefs as any belief that has a direct and long-term impact on how we perceive, understand, and express ourselves, generally which was learned early in life.

What do you think there Eva, are you ready for "an upgrade?" Would you like to feel happier, healthier, and more confident?

I sure am and this is an area I have always found this area very perplexing. I recognize that some thoughts keep repeating in my mind, making a theme in my life, but are they all core beliefs or are there other kinds?

Over my thirty some years of exploring the human mind, I have come to believe that there are differing levels of beliefs. There are what I will call, for differentiation sake, core beliefs, strong beliefs and fleeting beliefs. I believe that every belief we develop has a direct connection with, or is, at least impacted by core beliefs.

You know me, examples please.

Here's an example of a strong belief: when a man and a woman are walking together down the street, they might believe that the man should always walk closest to the road. Another one would be that a man should open the door for a lady when she gets in or out of the car. They may be life-long beliefs, but neither directly influences the person's basic perception or understanding of how they live their lives.

An example of a fleeting belief could be, "I can't play guitar." This would be particularly true during the first stage of trying to learn the instrument. Once a certain level of learning has been achieved, the thought would not arise again because the mind automatically knows the belief is wrong ...although some days?

A new belief will replace this one as a higher level of achievement is accomplished. Then the belief might be something like, "I can play a few songs on my guitar."This evolution could keep evolving until I am a regular guest on the Grand Old Opry," if that is where I set my goals.

This situation actually happened in my life. I received a guitar for Christmas, the year I turned 14. I bought myself some books, so I could learn to play. Not having much money, lessons were not readily available to me, so I learned some songs by teaching myself. With no natural sense of rhythm or ear for music, it seemed that I was competing with cats sitting on the fence at midnight screeching at the moon ... and often won.

One afternoon, being determined to learn just one song well, I played my guitar and sang for about two hours solid. Rather than being supportive, my mother barged into my room and threw a portable tape recorder on my bed as she yelled at me, "Listen to yourself. This is what we have to put up with!"

To further imbed a lack of confidence in my musical skills, there were often snide remarks from other members of my family regarding my lack of musical skill. It was a big joke to them. My feelings really got hurt!

I persevered throughout my life, plugging away at songs, slowly getting better but never really gained any confidence until, one day a miracle happened!

A friend gave me an electronic guitar tuner for Christmas. I immediately discovered that my guitar had been tuned too low all these years and had forced my voice into an unnatural range. By improving the tuning of the guitar, my voice gradually improved to being quite pleasant and more than tolerable.

To deal with the belief, "I am not good enough to sing or play guitar well." (The real core belief being just plain, "I am not good enough.") I joined a Karaoke group. It was pretty shaky at first but after a year of singing, with a lot of perseverance and many anxious moments, I am now considered quite a good singer. I feel a lot better about my singing…and about myself. Nashville has not knocked on my door yet, but any day now.

At least my fleeting beliefs have matured as my singing and guitar playing have improved. It just took a little time, about 35 years! Now I can deal with the core beliefs. Isn't it amazing how the things we learned as kids can make such a mess when we are older? I sure am glad there are tools available for getting these things sorted out!

Because of my background in metaphysics and energy medicine, I believe I take a fairly radical view on how our minds work in comparison to more conventional standards. I stand to be corrected by anyone who would care to prove me wrong, but I put forth the theory that there are only two basic needs from which all core beliefs stem.

I am safe   I am loved.

There are many core beliefs. They will vary from person to person, but they will always flow back to the basic needs of safety and love.

Do we all have the same set of core beliefs?

No. We all have the same basic needs to be safe and loved. However, we would only have the same core beliefs if we all viewed being safe and loved in the same way. However, since we don't, the beliefs we develop in the process of learning our version of safety and love, this is called living life, is where our differences begin. Even twin children will still have different views of life and boundary requirements.

Another factor affecting the development of core beliefs is our environmental conditions; where we live, how we live, and with whom.

Compare these two situations; let's say you were a child raised in a home where your parents loved each other openly and positively. There was an abundance of demonstrated affection for each other and for you. Would your view of safety and love be the same or different than that of the child who was raised by only one parent, who left him regularly with a baby sitter because it took two jobs to keep a roof over their heads?

I can certainly relate to that. I still carry a painful memory of back in Austria when I was about two or three years old. I was going for a long ride with my dad on his bike that seemed to take forever. I was happy. I loved being with my dad.

After some time, however, we stopped at a building (that I would describe today as looking like an institution). Once inside, my dad exchanged pleasantries with a lady then came over to me, kissed me good-bye, and left.

This lady took me to a large room with about twenty beds. Here, another woman was telling a bedtime story a group of children. Since there was no bed for me, so I was tucked in with another little girl. I was in total shock.

The next day was hard. I wouldn't eat or participate in any of the activities. Since my dad came to visit that very evening, I'm sure they had told him how I was feeling. He talked, I listened. Who knew anything about communication skills? Dad talked a lot about how nice this place was. (Actually for the 1940's, this establishment was very posh. It even had a swimming pool.) But I felt so very sad when my dad left again without me.

I don't recall how long I was at this place, likely about three weeks. Questions kept begging to be answered in my little head; what did I do wrong? why don't they want me at home any more?

My core beliefs that developed around this whole situation, I believe are: I am not loved and I do not belong to anyone. Going to another level, I recognize that I have a strong need for security and independence. I do not leave myself at risk especially around other people. I do not want to chance being hurt again.

I realize now, how these beliefs have limited my life. I am glad to be able to finally realize them, so I can begin to make some positive changes that will help me find more happiness.

Looking back at this situation from my parents' point of view, they certainly got what they considered the finest place in the community to care for me. I do not know the circumstances that led them to put me there during this time. Judging by the quality of the home, they certainly loved me. Unfortunately, from my mind as a three year old, my conclusions were very different.

Isn't it interesting to look back at your life and see how what you learned has affected you? Can you see how your "core beliefs" stem from the desire to satisfy the two basic needs, safety and love?

I believe that when we are born, being safe and being loved are our only two concerns. We do not know these needs consciously. They are innate drives that force us to take part in life in pursuit of their satisfaction. It is only once they are satisfied that we truly come to terms with ourselves, allowing us to advance perceptibly in our own personal growth. They can only be satisfied by getting past our belief systems that keep us in protective safety.

There is a paradox in the above statement, in that we seem to have to work really hard to maintain safety and love. Yet, in truth, we are born with them as intrinsic parts of our design. Our life choices, based on our core beliefs, are what separate us from the truth of who we really are, until such time as we abandon the falsities, work through our smoky glass and return to safety and our true nature of love.

We are born into safety, then trained out of it!

Why are safety and love the only primary needs? How do we know when we are truly safe?

True safety is primary because, without it, love cannot be expressed in its truest form. Through the effect of protective safety, any interactions will be guarded and distorted, and might be expressed as guilt, hate, remorse, greed or other undesirable emotions.

Knowing you are truly safe and comfortable with yourself allows you to choose how you express yourself so you can relax and enjoy life more completely. It allows you to live in grace.

We know we are truly safe when we feel relaxed and confident, with our mind at ease. We have no need, at any level, to have to protect ourselves from anything because being truly safe is a natural state.

We have unlearned true safety through our life experience.

Love is also a primary need as people, by nature, are gregarious. In other words, we naturally like hanging out with each other. Pure love also helps to increase our vitality, which keeps us healthy. We feel connected, a part of our group. The connectedness empowers us. We share in love by openly exchanging energy in the forms of touching, talking, etc. with each other. Our friends, lovers, children and other family members are all essential in our lives to satisfy our need for love.

Love is a positive force, the one and only true driving force of the universe and the basis for everything that exists.

Love helps us to maintain a healthy, balanced life style. So why are safety and love the only common denominators, the primary needs?

All the roads in our lives lead back to safety and love.

Can you give an example of how a core belief relates to safety and love?

Let's pretend that you have a brother who is five years older than you. To you, little sister, Mom and Dad constantly give him more attention than you get. From this perception, you develop a belief that "brother is more important than me." That belief further translates into a belief that "men are more important than women." The basis of your belief is your desire to be loved fully and completely by your mom and dad, your primary source of love as a child.

Since you feel that you are not being loved as much as your brother is, you develop a core belief that you are not lovable. This misperception could distort your view of love, and create your love pattern. The great concern here is that if the belief is strong enough, as an adult, you will attract relationships with men who support this belief.

Doesn't sound promising, does it? Where does this leave you?

Not receiving the love and respect that should be mine!

Right! Here are some of the core beliefs that may develop. Can you relate to these feelings?

- Men are more lovable than women.

- Men hold more power than women.

- I am second rate to men.

- I need to be independent of men if I am to be powerful.

Core beliefs that are non-supportive such as this one actually block valuable information from presenting itself in our conscious minds. If the information is distorted, we cannot act on it clearly. Although the intention in our mind is to keep us safe, it dramatically limits our access to new knowledge and the phenomenal life we really deserve. We may actually find that many of the beliefs we base our lives on, are formed from completely unsubstantiated and incorrect information, tainting our lives for no real or valid reason.

We live according to our belief systems... right or wrong.

As you likely found out later, your brother often appeared to be getting more attention only because your mom and dad were helping him with schoolwork and giving him instructions on his chores. They did not mean to appear to "love him more." Brother just was at a more evolved social level than you, that required more time and attention from them. Nobody ever intended to make you feel less loved than anybody else!

We all have the natural desire to feel safe. It is likely that not only did you not feel as loved as your brother, but the situation also left you feeling unsafe since your parents were your dominant source of love. You might have feared that you were dispensable in the eyes of your parents. If this situation occurred repeatedly, in your mind it would have become "the way it is" in your life.

This factor is called familiarity patterning. This belief, created in protective safety, would compel you as an adult, to attract relationships with men who leave you feeling less than them or you might just keep unconsciously opting out of relationships as they become too scary. This is a familiar pattern and thus a safe one for you. Isn't it amazing how a completely innocent situation can create such a potentially destructive belief?

Since knowledge and experience are the two most valuable tools we have, it is of extreme importance that we are diligent in developing conscious self-awareness followed by taking action. Once we recognize a non-supportive belief, it is truly in our best interest to change the outcome, and the belief. The action of changing the outcome causes an increase in personal power, by releasing the congested energy of the old thought pattern.

Let me see if I understand this correctly by using a different situation. As I was growing up, I learned to recognize the habitual reactions of one of my parents when they were expressing anger. The reaction that I learned was that I just

needed to stand back and be quiet, make myself invisible. Then I knew I was safe.

As an adult, this belief automatically tells me that when I am interacting with someone who is expressing anger, I need to stand back and be quiet in order to feel "safe." Through my discussions with you, I now know this is an act of protective safety. I can see that if I am to continue using this protective device, I am really preventing myself from moving forward and I am limiting fulfilment in my life. I know that I need to choose true safety and love myself enough to speak up when I need to. Is this what you mean?

You are exactly right, my friend, I think you are getting the picture!

Can you give some other examples of supportive and non-supportive beliefs?

Sure, some non-supportive beliefs are:
- Money is evil
- Watch out for policemen, they will put you in jail
- Skinny is beautiful
- I am stupid
- I mustn't use my imagination, because I don't want to look stupid
- Nobody loves me... and many more

There are literally hundreds of non-supportive beliefs. All of these statements flow back to deep-seated feelings and core beliefs seated in the feelings and memories that support the belief that one is not safe or not loved. Any belief that undermines the value of any person would be considered non-supportive.

That's a little scary. Can you warm up with some supporting beliefs?

Supporting beliefs could include:

- I know I am a beautiful, loving person
- I love myself
- I do what is best for me in the long run
- I base my body weight on how I feel in my body
- I deserve to be respected
- I treat all others with respect
- I am safe
- I am loved

These beliefs also flow back to core beliefs resulting from one's healthy perspective of safety and love.

The bottom line with core beliefs is that we need to be aware of our beliefs and how they affect our lives. We need to be willing to risk making any changes we deem necessary .....and then take action.

Only we can improve our own situation. It is the only way we can ever have true peace of mind.
Here's another part of my life I find perplexing. I find it really hard to stay away from sweets. Does that have a belief basis?

Not only does it have a belief basis, but it also has

emotions tied to it. Any type of excess keeps a person's mind off balance. This allows them unconsciously to maintain emotional imbalance, which is a protective safety device. The mind develops the excuse to not look at what is promoting the need for the excessive sweets to start with. It becomes a vicious circle. You eat the sweets because you feel off balance; the sweets cause the imbalance to be perpetuated by throwing the body's metabolism off. The endocrine system tries to compensate for the imbalance from the sweets and the feelings, which again perpetuates the imbalance and allows the mind to not deal with the issue that started it all. Later on, we will discuss how core beliefs affect our bodies and our health.

Do we know what the core belief and the emotions are?

Any types of sweets eaten to excess usually relate back to a lack of "sweetness" in life. Candies are an artificial stimulant. They lift the user from a "low" and create a simulated "high." The need for artificial stimulation would have been learned as a child. This is a safety issue that is tainted by lack of love, as well. Likely, you were told that you were "being stupid" or misbehaving, that your ideas were fanciful and that you should smarten up and "get real."

Due to a fear, and later guilt, of expressing your imagination and your innate love for beauty, you felt unsafe and therefore needed to hold in your true feelings. When these feelings were held back, they stayed inside your body lowering the quality of overall energy and possibly wreaking havoc until they are released.

Our creative energies, like our sex drives are very powerful. It is natural for us to express them, and not to hold them back. The holding back or expressing through a distortion of our natural drives is one of the biggest problems we face in life. It is the basis for many unacceptable and often illegal actions.

Physically, the pancreas is the organ which has to do with the flow of insulin or sweetness in the body. As the belief system became stronger inside the self, the functioning of the pancreas decreases. The mind, in an attempt to balance the functions of the body, causes a craving for sweets, so that the love of life can be felt, albeit artificially. Unfortunately, there are many side effects to be reckoned with such as obesity and diabetes. Another consideration with the problem of over indulgence is the old Pavlovian theory of positive reinforcement.

How many times, as a child, do you recall your parents saying something like this? "If you are good today, I will take you out for some ice cream?" This often repeated action instils a belief that if you do something "good," you deserve a reward. Sound familiar? Can you equate the eating of sweets with the need for recognition?

I recall that one for sure. Do all uncomfortable situations in life have core beliefs attached to them?

Every situation in life has core beliefs attached to it.

This is a bold statement but nonetheless true. We attract what we know, and what we don't know does not stay in our lives, unless we come to know it. What is important is that many of the uncomfortable situations we have in our lives can be dealt with and changed. I feel adamant that too much of our lives are limited only because we believe we are powerless to do anything about the situation.

When we become aware of new possibilities, our knowing changes and so does the experience we base our decisions on.

Is there a technique to knowing when a core belief is occurring?

Earlier, if you recall, when discussing protective safety, I indicated that it is important to pay attention to what you are feeling in your body. For example, if you feel your breath becoming shorter and more rapid or your muscles tightening while your mind is caught up in a single repetitive thought, you are in protective mode. The body responses are a signal indicating that a core belief that has been activated.

How do I know what the core belief is?

Listen to the theme in your mind. What thought keeps recurring? What are you telling yourself? You can discover your core beliefs by paying close attention to the "I," "You" and "He's and she's" in your self talk. For example: "I am so…" (Note that this phrase is the path to the core belief, not the core belief itself.)

In this example, he feels angry, (Core belief- I am not worthy), which we learned earlier is a socially acceptable way of showing fear. He is likely feeling fear because she is his supply of love. He fears his supply of love is being cut off. He protects himself by getting angry. When she arrives, ten minutes late and explains she made a wrong turn, his anger will dissipate and be replaced by other safer thoughts. The base core belief is "I feel unsafe" because "I am unlovable."

Is there a way I can identify core beliefs during self-exploration?

This is the primary purpose of witness consciousness. Learn to stand back; watch and listen to yourself as you go through your day. Pay attention to your body reactions. Listen for any thoughts that are directed to your perception of yourself. Core beliefs will often start with "I am." They are a statement to yourself telling you how you do life right now. How many times in a day do we tell ourselves; "I am …," only to have the process sped up and multiplied when life goes awry?

Strong beliefs that are based on the "I am" statement begin with expressions that include words like "can't," "don't" and the all-time favourite: "should." "I shouldn't eat so many sweets" is a good one, "I can't do that" or "I don't deserve that."

Can I deal with changing the core belief during a difficult situation?

There are three concerns for you to recognize when dealing with core beliefs and the supporting drama when you are in the midst of a storm. First is that you do not feel safe because of a perceived threat, so there is little likelihood of being able to think clearly and rationally. Secondly, the emotional intensity created in the situation over-magnifies the belief, depending on the intensity of the situation.

Thirdly please recognize that we are our own main audience. We listen to ourselves constantly, whether we know we are listening or not. We cannot escape hearing our beliefs every single time they blare out like an old foghorn. When we are engaged in an emotional situation, we do not have the conscious capability of making healthy changes, so we must until the situation has settled back down.

Try to pay attention to what you are saying to yourself so that you can prepare to make changes when the event is done. Remember you are the only person who has to listen to what you say 24 hours per day, seven days per week. No coffee breaks. During these emotionally charged situations, you will be most likely to encounter some core beliefs.

What is the best way to deal with a core belief in this situation?

The first action, and this one takes time and awareness to implement, is to recognize when a core belief reaction is starting to occur. Immediately ensure your physical safety, then, tell yourself that you are safe. Take a series of three deep breaths, slowly in and out repeating "I am safe and protected" with each breath. Tell yourself that you are not the thoughts you are having, and that you will choose other thoughts instead when you are able. See yourself in your mind's eye, separate from the thoughts. You are you. Your thoughts are just thoughts. Try to relax and feel what is going on. Let the feeling move down your body into the earth. Know you are safe. Relax. The thoughts and feelings have no power over you. Once you have released it, and you are feeling calmer, you can analyze it if you want and try to understand what it was really telling you. Then you can make changes.

Now that you can consciously choose the outcome, think about it and decide, what the result is you desire. Aim for consistency in your result. Each time you engage in a situation:

Teach yourself to stop automatically reacting.
Implement your new choice instead.

This process takes practice. Do not get angry or frustrated with yourself because you do not act exactly the way you want. Give yourself the space and love to retrain yourself gradually. Let yourself have the privilege of making a few mistakes. Just do your best. It took you a long time to learn the original belief, so it will take time to accept the new one. The need for being perfect is a protective safety mechanism. Do not buy into it. Do your best for the level you are at and you will gradually learn to be in control.

There is another way of explaining this process as well. There are four steps:

- Become consciously aware of the situation that is developing.

- Sit in it -Don't avoid the thoughts and feelings. Accept them as part of your present circumstances. Do not act out or validate the thoughts.

- Make the choice concerning how you desire the new outcome to be

- Implement the choice

- Most important; remember that you are not the situation!

That all sounds fine and dandy when I have time to choose how to respond. But what about situations like this:

I deal with a lot of people at work. Let's say someone comes at me requesting an immediate answer. They appear to be very confrontational. I don't have time to go through these four steps. At this time, my first concern is to deal with the matters at hand. During this stressful event, how can I concentrate on which core belief is going off? Or what possibly can I do about this situation?

Try to stay conscious of how you interact with this person. The words are not so important, nor are the actions. It is how you feel that is your clue. The feeling will give you the key to the core belief. You can work on the key after the situation is finished and dealt with. The goal during the interaction is just to not respond to the old impulses.

Once you begin to understand the core belief that triggered the feeling, you can begin to make appropriate changes over the next few times a similar interaction occurs. You can play with events like this, trying out different outcomes until you find one that works for you. Then you just repeat that one any time you need it. Keep in mind that you will want to create an outcome based in the spirit of love. It creates the best safety for all.

Be watchful when working with your core beliefs. They can be powerful statements that may have strong emotions attached to them. They have been with you for a very long time and may resist being thwarted. This is why the issue about personal safety was presented first. Deal with changing a core belief when you are in true safety, not while you are in the midst of a total melt down.

If you can train yourself how to use tools to keep yourself cool when you are calm, they will be useful for you when those situations occur at times when self control is challenged.

Remember: If the issue feels too big for you to deal with on your own, get some help from a professional!

❧

Tell me more about the "resist being thwarted" part.

When a core belief has strong emotion attached to it, the mind also has a strong attachment to maintenance of the belief. The ego likes things to stay the same. The ego identifies with the emotional charge of the belief and believes that if you change the belief, it may be endangered in some way. Because of this fear factor, the ego will do everything it can to prevent the change. As you are trying to change the outcome of the belief, the egoic mind may set up roadblocks in order to maintain its status quo.

Do you remember the very first time you came over to my home?

Boy, do I ever! I decided that I did not want to be alone this particular night, so I phoned you. When you answered the phone, you said that a bunch of friends were over playing cards and that I should come over and join in on the fun. I felt nervous, but after a few minutes of thinking, I decided "Why not?"

I felt that I was really stepping out of my comfort zone.

So, what happened on your way over?

On the way there, I decided I wanted a piece of gum. I reached for my purse only to discover that I had left it at home and it was too far to go back and get it. To add to the dilemma, and in my absolute horror, I looked at my gas gauge. It was on the "E." Boy was my ego acting out!

Even, with no money and no driver's license, I trudged on. I had never been to your place before, what should have been a 30-minute trip took me over an hour. I must have hit every red light and made every wrong turn possible. I was a wreck by the time I got to your place. Luckily, I was not stopped by the police and didn't run out of fuel.

What was the key decision that weakened the strength of the core belief for you? How has it affected your life?

The key decision was to persevere and keep going to make it to your place regardless of my apprehension. In the past, I would have just turned around and gone back home or more likely, I just would not have started out at all. I am glad I did make it to your place. It showed me that I could do it, and I had a great evening. Now instead of refusing new adventures, I accept them so I can grow through the challenges they present.

I figure that if I made it through that night, I can make it through anything.

I am glad you did finally make it. You set off lots of my core beliefs. No, that's not true; your events set up the conditions for me to see some of my own core beliefs.

The essential thing to remember when making any changes in your life is to ensure your personal safety first. There is no room for heroes in this process. Get to know your place of oneness with yourself and learn how to get there when things get "iffy." When you can comfortably keep yourself in your strength there will be less emotional turmoil for you to endure.

The process takes a while, so be good to yourself. Take your time and enjoy the ride. Give yourself the opportunity to be a person in growth mode, and leave room for mistakes. They can be fun if you let them... and a good tool for personal growth.

Living in your Core Beliefs

In the previous chapter, we chatted about what Core Beliefs are and how they affect our lives in specific situations. Now, let's talk about core beliefs and their function in everyday life.

There is nothing that occurs in our lives that is not affected in some way by our belief systems. Human beings are emotional animals. Every factor of our life is affected by our emotions. Our emotions and our beliefs are very strongly intertwined. Even the macho man that does not express emotion is still strongly affected by the emotions he restrains within himself. We see everything through our emotions. They directly affect our view of the world, much like the way we would see it if we held a piece of smoky glass in front of our eyes. We cannot see what is on the other side of the glass (our emotions) without its interference.

"Our reality" is how we view life through our smoky glass (our emotional patterns). Our reality is unique to us alone, because it is filtered through our emotions and beliefs. It is an interesting fact of life that we may have billions of realities while there is only one "actuality."

Actuality is the way it is
Reality is the way we perceive the way it is

Can you give me an example? That sounds like a pretty big topic.

A few years ago, a friend of mine was wishing to purchase a house on acreage in a very specific area, near where we live. She found a house that she felt met her needs. She was extremely excited with her find and was determined to purchase this property immediately. Her reality was that this find was her "gateway to Nirvana." She envisioned moving in, gardening and living her "back-to-the-earth" lifestyle without another worry in the world. However, an inspection of the property revealed that, in actuality, this was not such a "golden find." The property was situated on a hard, slopey rocky terrain which was regularly subjected to flooding during the rainy season. The excess water caused the house to reek of mould and mildew. There was actually very little arable land for her garden. Even once the actuality of the situation was pointed out to her, she held on tight to "her reality." She was determined that she and her chickens were destined to live out their lives in her dream home on this property. Fortunately for her, in my opinion, the property sold before she could put in an offer. It would have been a very expensive lesson in reality versus actuality.

Our best defense is to understand the difference between actuality and reality, and how we see life through recognizing "our reality," at any given time. This is getting back to the witness consciousness we talked about earlier.

If we can step back and watch ourselves, we will soon observe patterns which occur that affect our good decision making abilities. These emotional patterns are set off by core beliefs. They are the same core beliefs that have been participating in our lives since they first developed way back when we were little guys. They didn't really serve us well then, and they sure won't serve us well now (except for the good ones, of course!). When we see them acting out, we can take steps to change our expression of them.

Wouldn't you agree that one of the most important lessons in this conversation is accepting that we can never know actuality? We are always dealing with reality because our perception is tainted by our emotions and belief systems. Even though I was able to point out some realities about the property my friend wanted to buy, we still may not have known the actuality.

To appease our egos, I would just say that if we can accept that everything we see in our lives is filtered though our emotions and beliefs and that the perception is subject to change as our interpretation of the related information changes, we will do just fine. It is what makes life interesting and us human.

If we view the activities in our lives as a detached observer when we are trying to make decisions, we will make better decisions because we let the investment in the situation go until we can clearly access as much good information needed for making the decision.

I am sure that my friend would have gladly let go of that property, not the dream, once she would have let go of the emotional entanglement she put herself in.

Wow, that really is important to understand the difference isn't! I never thought of it that way before.

As I stated earlier, core beliefs affect every moment of our lives. They affect every one of us and interestingly enough, in exactly the same way. However, our expression of them will be as individual as we are. As a medical intuitive, I work with people every day, in the hopes of helping them to live healthier expressions of their lives.

When I scan their bodies, and I feel congested energy, I know the root cause by the organ(s) which are affected. By asking a few simple but pointed questions I can very quickly find the cause of the concern and help the client "make a shift."

This understanding of the body energy is very similar to the "yin & yang" of Traditional Chinese Medicine. My intention is always to find and eliminate the blockage in the natural flow of body energy, caused by core beliefs so the related energy flows more freely. After all, the better the energy flows on any level the healthier we are overall.

One particular client I worked with had concerns about a compressed disc in her thoracic region (upper back). This had bothered her for many years. Short of surgery, she had been told by the medical professionals that she would just have to tough it out. There was nothing else to be done.

As I observed her telling me about it, I saw a picture in my mind's eye, of her as a child, with her father standing over her. He was aggressively belittling her in a very loud, dominating tone. She was terrified since, in her eyes, her father was a huge person and more importantly, her protector. In her mind, she felt threatened by the one person who should have kept her safe. Her emotional reaction to the situation was that she needed to protect herself, by doing what I call "turtle-shelling." She tried to pull her head into her body. This often repeated reaction caused excess pressure on her T-4 vertebra. The affecting core beliefs (her smoky glass) in this matter were: I am not safe, I am not safe with people "bigger" than me, and I am not safe around loud, dominating people.

This became a continuing pattern in her life, so, as a result, in adult life; she attracted non-assertive men because she felt safe with them, and, whenever in the presence of dominating people, she cowered.

Neither of these choices gave her much satisfaction. Eventually, due to the constant pressure of pulling her head into her body, she manifested the problem in her neck. Through a combination of exercises, both physical and energetic, in conjunction with further discussions about how she interacts with her father and other dominating people; the situation is becoming much more manageable. As she learned to separate herself from her memories, by using witness consciousness, the pressure released in her neck, so it is no longer irritating. She now is learning to stand tall"(again, the result of awareness).

In a similar situation, a male client had difficulty in relating with his father. He felt completely undermined in his own essence, since the belief he learned was that he could never meet his father's expectations and "everything he tried to do was wrong." His reaction was to give up on his own male energy (the energy of taking action). This choice manifested an existence where he achieved few of his life's dreams. He endured a lifetime career far below his potential. Eventually, he developed a very serious case of skin cancer (because he could not tolerate being touched by life). The saddest part of this story was that he continued to uphold his existing belief patterns and turned away from any help resulting in premature death.

Can you see the similarities and differences in these examples? Both people had come to realize some childhood issues were apparent, in their adult lives. Both had manifested physical and emotional challenges due to their beliefs. However, the difference lies in the fact that only one chose to work them through and find a new level of peace and personal strength.

The reason there was a difference in the visible effect of their core beliefs (issues prior to treatment) was based on the combination of the core beliefs that expressed at the time. The process is very similar to the computer analogy. Each belief is like a software program. The human mind is so powerful that several of them can go off simultaneously. In fact, our mind is so good at it, that when similar situations occur, the same set will be triggered each time. The mind, in both of the individuals previously mentioned, created a reaction to keep them safe according to the beliefs it contained, while at the same time it magnetized opportunities that repeated the same experience over and over (mental conditioning that creates our perception of life).

The difference in how they each dealt with their situations was due to their own free choice. Nobody is obligated to make changes. However, we always have to live with our choices.

A person develops survival skills early in life and then uses these coping mechanisms in their own unique way to adapt throughout their life. Even siblings will have differing beliefs about life and will have different methods for protecting themselves.

Being able to watch yourself in a detached manner will help you to determine what your coping mechanisms are. If life has been consistently unsafe, you may find yourself constantly in protective mode. You might learn to be very sensitive with a low tolerance for pain of any kind. Your skills will likely cause you to react disproportionately even to minimal stimulus, so that you appear to be a victim in constant need of emotional support.

Someone else may pull inside themselves, becoming cold like a stone. Their motto becomes "Nobody can hurt me." Unfortunately, no one can get in to warm them up either. Everyone has core beliefs that evoke feelings of lack of safety.

How do you keep safe?

Knowing how you protect yourself is definitely something worth exploring.

Core beliefs are a fact. We will always have them. Fortunately, because of two important aspects of the filing system in our brains, we can take charge of our lives and make changes. Firstly, we all have healthy core beliefs, intermingled with the ones that create our life challenges. Secondly, by separating ourselves from the unhealthy beliefs, we can learn to recognize uncomfortable situations, work through them and ultimately choosing healthier outcomes.

How we react to or respond to our beliefs directly affects our quality of life.

What are some examples of everyday situations where core beliefs impact our choices?

Let's take some really safe situations. How about our living conditions and careers, etc?

In my case, having a place to come home to is very important. As a child, my parents were constantly in transit. I was an adult before I ever lived in one place for more than three years. I learned to adapt quickly but rarely felt settled in any place.

My core beliefs were:

- Don't get too settled, because you will be moving soon anyway,
- Everything is temporary, so it's not safe to let yourself get too close or attached to anybody or anything
- Running away is easier than facing challenging situations.

I do not like changing residences and I don't like to run away from things, but I recognize there is an urge to run whenever life appears to be a struggle. I actually lose about 10 lbs each time I move, just from the nervousness.

I have lived in apartments, condos, big houses and small houses, anywhere as long as it I can call it home.

I am a real homebody; so, one of my dreams is to finally find a home where I can stay put for the rest of my life. Since I now recognize the core beliefs at play, I can work through them and look at what is really bothering me instead of doing my habitual pattern of moving frequently. (My longest stay has been 11 years so far.)

Are you ready to do some work for yourself?

Here's an opportunity for you to do some introspection.

- Why do you live where you do?
- How important is your home to you?
- Do you consider yourself to be a home body?
- Do you consider your house to be big or small?
- Is it a townhouse, apartment or single detached house?
- Is it located on a busy street, a quiet cul-de-sac or nestled out in a beautiful spot in the country?
- How do you keep your home?

As you answer each of these questions, try to determine the reason for your choices. Each part of your statement has a belief inherent to it. You will learn a great deal about yourself through this investigation and will likely see some patterns.

Isn't it great to learn more about yourself at a new level? Eva and I hope you are acquiring some valuable new tools to guide yourself and to find more happiness in your life.

By the way, there are no right or wrong answers.

- If you live in a big house, was it because you lived in a similar house as a child?
- Or is this your home now because you felt you needed the security that a big house provides?
- Do you need to impress the world with your possessions?

Gosh, this statement really stirred up a reaction in me. In my 30's, I had a beautiful home on acreage with a stream running at the front of it. I always remember how very proud I was when someone came over. Looking back, I realize the whole situation was about emotional security for me.

I believe I was asking unconsciously, "Aren't I so very successful?" "Didn't I do good?" "Didn't we do well financially?"

My insecurities about not being good enough got an "externally fix" momentarily with each compliments about my beautiful house.

Here are some more questions to explore in order to gain some insights for yourself:

- Do you live in a small house because it is cozy or because it is all you can afford?

- Do you live on a busy street because it's like the house in which you grew up?
- Is this location so loud that you "can't hear yourself think?"
- Do you live in a big city because it is "what you know?"
- Or do you have no concept or belief system about life in the country, so you have never gravitated to the rural scene to discover that set of possibilities?
- What keeps you where you are?
- Who do you live with?
- Who decided you were to live there?

There are many more questions you can ask yourself that are related to your home that will help you understand yourself more. Can you come up with any?

Careers are much the same.

- What is your vocation?
- Does your job involve a lot of interaction with people?
- Did you have a lot of people in your life as a child?
- What do you do with people?
- How do you have your needs satisfied in your job?

Is there a parallel between today's interfacing with others and how you lived as a child?

I heard there was a comparative study done that indicated a strong similarity between the teacher's remarks a person got in grade one and in grade twelve. And we call this progress? Do you see how this relates to the (non) progression of core beliefs?

Look at the components that characterize your job.

- Do you work with your hands?

- Do you work with computers?

- Where did you learn your personal skills that determined your career in this field?

- How much education did your job require?

- Do you have a mentor whom you are emulating?

- What components make your job unique to others?

- What is your attraction to the company you are with?

- Why do you do the job you do?

- Is it the same as one of your parents?

- Do you do this job because you like it, or because you fell into it, or because it pleases your parents?

- How long have you been doing your job?

- Do you still enjoy it? What keeps you going back?

- Is it a pleasure vehicle for you or simply security?

We eat, sleep and play what we have learned as children.

- How different is the food you eat today from what you ate as a child?

- What foods do you use as "comfort foods?"
- What are your beliefs about sleep?
- What position do you fall asleep in?
- What gives you comfort when life gets tough?

One of my fondest memories that gives me much comfort was that of my grandma. We lived in an old house; Dad, Mom, Grandma and me. It had a wood stove that Grandma kept stoked all day to heat the house. Each day, she warmed a red brick in the oven and at night, she would wrap it in a fuzzy little towel, and then place it in my bed, as she tucked me in. How I loved my Grandma as I dozed off to sleep snuggled in my warm little nest. I remember fondly how that old red brick made me feel so loved.

Today, whenever I am feeling out of sorts, I like to curl up in my bed with my red, hot water bottle. It reminds me of the warmth and security I felt as a child, and the love for my Grandma. Memories like these certainly evoke good core beliefs. I find they are so important for getting through the tough times. Can we deny the existence of any core beliefs?

Core beliefs do not need us to give them recognition in order to operate. They are automatic. Denying our core beliefs would be about the same as driving our car in heavy traffic, pretending there are no rules necessary for keeping us safe. Core beliefs are our perpetual guardians. They stimulate our protective safety devices. They reside in our egos ever watchful to keep us alive. Without them, our lives would be very short indeed, for the first time we faced danger, we would likely be killed.

It is only through recognizing and reprogramming our belief systems, that we can change the way we protect ourselves. By striving to live continually in true safety, we can be more open and expansive, as we experience life. Getting beyond the unconscious control of our core beliefs is the only way to create permanent change. This requires being (witness) conscious of how our mind plays the game we call our life.

Core beliefs are the rules.

Does dealing with our core issues have to be painful?

Ideally, the answer is no, however, until we can incorporate a reasonable level of true safety, the process is likely to be painful in some circumstances. It really depends on what the issue is, how attached we are to it and what we get out of keeping it active.

There is a learned tendency for us to personalize traumatic situations. When an event occurs, we lose our identity in it. Through detachment, we can maintain our identity as the event occurs, allowing us to stand back and disengage the connection. After all, are we not more than these fleeting situations? They keep happening and we keep on going, so how can we possibly be the event? If we can let the pain belong to the event, rather than personalizing it, we can reduce the impact on our emotions and be more objective.

This sounds rather complicated.

It sounds like it, but it isn't really. Take a situation such as starting a new job. Many of us find this to be a particularly daunting time. As we prepare to start this important event, we feel our body getting tight and our breathing rapid and shallow. Our mind gets filled with all the negative thoughts it can imagine. We are terrified. Our mind tells us, that if we make one mistake we will be out the door, and back on the unemployment line. It is the same for all of us until we learn to manage the process better.

By detaching from the old core belief program and choosing witness consciousness instead, you realize that this is an event that incites riots in your head, so you purposely relax your mind and body ahead of time. You arrive prepared by intentionally creating your own safety and peace of mind. As you begin the new job, you regularly take slow deep breaths and remind yourself that you are capable of doing this job well. It may, however, take time to master. You recognize the fear feelings but you do not identify with them. As you become aware of stressors, you nip them in the bud because you are ready for them. Just watching yourself and getting to know the "real" you is so empowering.

Very soon, You are the master!
As you learn to see yourself separate from your thoughts and emotions, making changes will become easy and painless.

If you can step back and detach from the issue, it will be much easier to look at the issue as a thing....separate from your self. This reduces the angst or intensity. Emotion and core beliefs have a strong bond, so, as the belief is exposed, there may be an emotional release as well. Your ego may try to resist expressing any emotion for fear of losing its identity and control. Recognize that you are not your ego. Tell your ego it is safe for you to let go. It is not in danger.

A great mantra for you to repeat often:

I know that I am safe and protected.

A young boy was enjoying his childhood. He wiled away the hours throwing stones into a pond, collecting frogs and other miniature friends and sharing stories with his buddies. It was a grand life, he thought. Nothing could be better.

When he returned home one night, he found his mother slouched on the couch, sobbing uncontrollably. The boy immediately ran to his mother to comfort her. As the tears fell, she whispered to him, "I guess you are the man of the house now. Your father is gone."

The little boy stood up straight, immediately showing his willingness to take on the job. He was proud that his mother thought so much of him. He would show the world that he was a man who could look after her. Little did he know; this was the end of his childhood.

Many years later, seated in his counsellor's office, he fought to understand where his life had gone and why he struggled so hard to find pleasure outside of work. Why did he only attract women who could not stand on their own, always dependent on him? Why did work take so much of his time?

As he recalled the tears rolling from his mother's eyes, so many years before, his own tears fell. He recalled how proud his mother was of him, for the courage and dedication he maintained, as he looked after her. He recalled giving up his friends, as life had dictated to him that there was no more time for play.

As the memories rolled through his mind, he realized that he had learned "how to be the man of the house." It was a lesson he had learned well.

It was very hard to separate himself from his feelings of responsibility for his mother. But through diligence, he eventually made room for himself. He reviewed his attraction for needy people and learned that he had needs too. With counselling, and by understanding the related core beliefs, he, over time let himself be a free person and quit taking on other peoples' responsibilities. As the tears flowed, the healing seeped in, and a new person was born.

Let's look at some of the core beliefs that are expressed in this person's life. What beliefs are apparent to you? Remember that safety and the need to be loved will always be the root issue in any situation. When you see the belief, try to take it back to love or safety.

Here's my take. You may see others and that's good because we all see life differently and that's okay (our smoky glass). The important issue here is learning to understand the root cause of the result.

- You can't play and have friends... and be an adult.
- Women need to be taken care of; they are weak.
- Loving his mother and keeping her safe means working hard.

Can you see how each of these beliefs can relate back to the needs for safety and love?

Without coming to terms with the core beliefs that are active in one's life, the wheels will spin unceasingly. This is the Law of Attraction. With this man, he believed women are weak; therefore, there was no attraction between him and "strong" women. The "needy" ones were drawn to his complementary energy. We always attract what we want on the inside and whatever makes our beliefs seem true (the old reality thing again).

The expression of emotions is good and vital for our best well-being. We as humans, both male and female, need to express them. Sometimes, when life becomes overwhelming, the release of emotions can be scary. If a person is not used to dealing with their issues or expressing emotion, they may find it painful when they let go of formerly prohibited thoughts and feelings. Healing can only really begin when the emotions that have been held back are allowed to release and express, purging the body at a very deep level. When the deep, dark secrets finally come out, people often feel pain as the memories of the trauma and abuse come to light. This pain may be felt in the body, but the pain is attached to the memory. It does not belong in the present.

This statement is not meant to belittle the situation. It still hurts. However, if the person can understand that the secrets are just memories and they have no need to feel embarrassed or lessened by them, it will be easier for them to let go and find the true freedom they desire.

Getting beyond the emotion is necessary, in order to truly resolve the issue. Unexpressed emotions remain in the body. Learning to separate ourselves from the memory and the emotion is essential as the pain is only connected to the memory, not to you.

Good support through counselling is of vital importance especially if the issue is a big one. Only you will know that for sure. It is better to have the support of a professional for any concern that you don't feel you can handle the situation on your own.

Always make your personal safety the first consideration. I know that I am safe and protected.

This is definitely a time for setting aside the control measures of your ego. Dealing with a major issue may leave you feeling vulnerable. Please do what you need to, in order to protect yourself so you can heal and move forward. Not taking the steps to protect yourself will just set you up for more challenges and unnecessary pain. You may even find that you give up trying to fix the situation. Preparation beforehand is essential.

A woman came to me for counselling because she had a "frozen" right shoulder. This can be a very painful and limiting condition. She was reluctant to be open with me at first, but the pain was quite debilitating and she needed to be the use of her arm in her work. As we worked together, she relaxed and became more confident. The answers came quickly as she told me about her determination to be successful in her new business. It was in a very difficult industry filled with red tape and hostile adversaries. It required a great deal of focus and stamina, but she knew she could do it. She knew that she had to "put her shoulder" into it, in order to succeed. For five years she had pushed with great determination but with little return. Now her condition was causing even more resistance.

The shoulder energetically represents "carrying the weight of the world" while the right side of the body represents taking action. Can you see the similes to her words? Can you visualize how she was pushing against the odds with her shoulder as if she was pushing against a wall?

Through energy work and discussions about her fears of failing, we were able to develop a plan that was more manageable for her. Very soon, the pain was gone, as she relaxed into a less driven business plan. Her core beliefs about "not being good enough" and "not feeling safe" had become very evident. The shoulder muscles relaxed as she changed her attitude. New flexibility, both emotionally and physically, gave her renewed vitality and helped open her up to success.

If pain is regarded as a tool that gives us insight into our emotional state, rather than a condition of the body that needs to be covered up and gotten rid of, we can learn more about ourselves and make greater progress in healing. Although the pain sometimes needs to be controlled, looking at the lessons behind the pain is critical to truly healing. Whether it is a frozen shoulder, inflamed disc or any disease, they all have an emotional component that demands attention and healing. In order to heal these conditions and remove them from the body, one must put themselves first, over the demands of the world.

Is it ethical for us to put ourselves first? What about our responsibilities to others?

If we do not put ourselves first, nobody else will. It is absolutely imperative that we realize and accept that we must be first in our lives. We live with ourselves every minute of everyday from birth to death.

Putting ourselves first allows us to look after our own needs. Only we know what those are and how we want them satisfied. The question of ethics we should ask in these situations is; "How do I look after myself without compromising the expression of the rights of others?"

How can we even think of helping others if we are not in a healthy state ourselves?

If we live in true safety, we have no need to make others feel unsafe, for no one is really a threat to us. It is only when we live in fear that we feel we may hurt others.

This causes the belief that we should put others first. In true safety, we always come from the consciousness of love ... Love for ourselves and all others, the ultimate win-win situation..

If we feel that we should put others first or perhaps others feel they should be first in our lives, then there is a strong necessity to look at our core beliefs.

No person is more or less important or valuable than any other person, for any reason!

If we could all understand and accept this statement, life for everyone would be much easier. After all, in the spirit of love, we are all created equal.

Is this personal responsibility? Absolutely! It cannot be any other way. Every person is responsible for his or her own actions.

We are always responsible for our selves and our choices.

Only we can cause our life to be the way it is. We see life through our own understanding (smoky glass). The only way we can change our life is by understanding how we participate in life. If we avoid taking responsibility for ourselves, then we cannot make any effective changes. The more attention we give to changing our life (cleaning the glass?), the more we need to put ourselves first.

It truly is all about us!

If you are truly serious about making your life better, then taking responsibility for yourself is the first step, however, please make sure that you are taking responsibility for what is yours. Do not let guilt or any other ego measure cause you to make distorted choices. You are the only one responsible for making changes in your life.

Are we ever responsible for other people?

No. Every person is responsible only for himself or herself. We can choose to take responsibility for others in order to protect and guide them (emphasis on "guide"), but the bottom line is that they are still responsible for themselves. It's just like the stewardess tells us when we fly, you have to put your mask on first because if you can't breathe, you won't be able to help anyone else.

Even children, no matter how small, hold a degree of self-responsibility. A small baby will let his mom know when he is hungry or needs to be changed. That is self-responsibility.

Mom and Dad's responsibility in this matter is only to ensure his needs are met by providing food, love, guidance, etc for him until he is mature enough to do so for himself.

Would you elaborate on the aspect of responsibility and children? I feel this is too important to just brush over.

In my opinion, society has not placed the appropriate amount of conscious investment into the early training of our children. Too much effort has been placed on trying to mold a child's actions into acceptable forms that comply with the parent's beliefs about life.

The more functional investment would be to focus on creating and maintaining a positive, safe, enriched environment where children can comfortably investigate their surroundings and discover their own rules of life within the parameters of that safety zone.

I feel that Mom and Dad would reap far greater rewards from parenthood by consistently providing their offspring with consciously chosen examples of healthy living rather than attempting to "bully" their children into compliance.

In order for children to grow into healthy expressions, adults need to treat them like the powerful human beings they are while they consciously loved, guide, nurture and respect these works in progress.

Children also need to understand that they are less experienced in life and need to accept a submissive position in the structure of the family and decisions that affect them until they have the maturity to make their own decisions.

Adults also need to understand that the child does not have the experience or understanding and that it is their role to assist the child in developing a healthy, functional set of rules so eventually they will be able to manage their lives themselves.

Symbolically, the life of a young child should be like playing in a playpen. The walls of the playpen are boundaries. The space inside the walls of the playpen is the space to be free to explore. The child is safe while inside the real playpen. The parents need to develop and maintain a "playpen" in the rest of their world so the child can maintain safety throughout its daily activities.

Children need to know healthy boundaries that are created and maintained consistently through a desire of the caregivers to allow the child to know life through its own eyes in true safety. While the child is playing in its safety zone, the parent's role is to supervise and assist the child in managing their life in a safe and healthy manner that will also work for them outside the playpen.

In conclusion, I feel that anyone who is a parent, willingly or not, needs to accept and understand that they are the ones who must choose the environment in which their offspring will grow. Striving to manage the circumstances rather than attempting to control the effects is a far healthier and less stressful way for both parent and child. It takes two people to create a child and it takes two willing and able people to accept their role as parents and role models to raise the child effectively.

It is vitally important to remember that by learning to manage one's own life, any children involved will benefit through the role modeling.

What about blame?

To be blunt, blame is one of the biggest con jobs that ever existed. Blame is someone else's interpretation of the incident that has occurred. Usually someone, who does not want to take responsibility for their part in the event, will try to make someone else responsible by "blaming" them. Blame evokes guilt, which is a manipulation, and nothing else!

We may be responsible for a situation that has occurred. We might even be at fault, because we made some "bad" choices. Blame has no place in human interactions.

Four of us were playing cards one night, guys against girls. The girls were winning as usual. My partner had been in a testy mood since he had arrived. Neither he nor his wife had mentioned what was going on, but it was easy to see things were not going well with him. In his normal good humour, he would have taken the losses with a couple of jokes and some teasing from his wife. This night, however, as we lost hand after hand, his temper worsened. Finally as the last hand was laid down, the volcano blew. My friend began raising his voice, blaming her for the lousy evening he was having. She returned in kind blaming him for the state of her life. The evening was ruined for all of us. What started out as a good evening certainly didn't end that way.

Had these folks been more aware of their own feelings and taken steps to be self-responsible, they may have been able to take some time to look within themselves and discover what they were feeling. They, then could have discussed their concerns at the appropriate time, and resolved the issues in privacy. Failing that, they could have just cancelled the get-together until they were feeling more sociable.

If whatever happened had been dealt with more appropriately, the blaming would not even have occurred. Each person would have accounted for himself or herself.

A situation that has gone awry can only be remedied if all the parties involved have the intention of fixing the problem. Blame undermines integrity, since the person who is blaming is seeking to have someone else be responsible for his or her actions.

There is a social belief which I believe is good and vital for the comfort and survival of all, which says we need to look out for each other. After all, this would be a lonely planet if we did not reach out to each other as fellow travellers in this journey. This however, is still very different from being responsible for or needing to be in control of others. Every person needs to have the room to discover their own best path in this life. Denying another person's self-responsibility limits their ability to know themselves in their fullest power.

People who have learned to live in true safety, practice looking at their life from a detached perspective and they give other people the room to do likewise. They try to work through their issues as they arise by recognizing when fears, core beliefs and protective safety devices activate.

Understanding true safety allows them to step forth with a feeling of inner security and confidence, knowing they are able to manage the situation as it evolves and separate themselves from the activities in their mind. It also allows them to recognize and respect other people's motivations and give them room to evolve as human beings.

This high degree of personal safety allows them to participate in, explore and enjoy their lives on any level they choose.

Relationships

Every situation in life has its own unique set of challenges. Of any of the situations that occur, relationships have definitely got to provide the most opportunities for facing yourself and your "demons."

In this chapter, we are going to look at relationships and try to figure out; how and why we find ourselves in the situations we do.

It is absolutely crucial to understand that how we do relationships is a learned experience and essential to mastering our personal growth.

Our greatest learning resource is our parents. When we were little, everything our caregivers did told us about the "rules of life." Because we are born with a blank mind that desires to be filled, we accepted whatever we were offered as being the truth. Even once we were old enough to create our own reality; our prior learning still had an influence on us. Fortunately, now we can decide whether or not those truths work for us or not and if we want to keep or change them.

Why do we have relationships? Sometimes it seems that it would be much easier just to be by ourselves and forget about the hassle of being with others.

You are so right, my friend. Sometimes it would feel better if we could go off and be by ourselves, however, we cannot escape ourselves so it is probably best to stick around and deal with the situation.

By nature though, we like having other people in our lives, in one way or another. I feel the basis for this is because we are born into families. We are just used to having people sharing space with us. In fact, if it wasn't for people getting together we would not even be here!

Right from the getgo, we are surrounded by people. Throughout our lives, we rely on other people to satisfy our needs and to love, guide and protect us. Since we have become accustomed to this feeling, as we move into independent adult life we naturally desire to continue this familiar pattern by forming "families" of our own.

As grown ups, we tend to model the types of relationships we know to be familiar. If you look at the family dynamics of any person, you will notice a repetitive pattern simulating the life they knew as a child, at least until they gained the awareness we are talking about here.

Children who were valued as an important part of their family group tend to be more comfortable around other people. They are more independent and have less need for seeking attention from others. Valued children grow up feeling safe and loved. They have little need to draw excessive or negative attention to themselves. They know what their needs are and quietly go about finding their satisfaction in healthy, meaningful ways. This, of course, is separate from actions that we may interpret as negative which are really just parts of their discovering their world. Remember, they don't always know the "rules" yet.

Children, who receive inadequate or inappropriate validation in their formative years, are often motivated by an insatiable need for attention. The less validation they receive means the more acting out they do, in an attempt to find fulfilment. It is like a void inside them that constantly yearns to be filled.

In the 1970's, Thomas A. Harris, a psychotherapist, published "I'm Okay. You're Okay." In his book, he names the dynamic of this latter style of relationship as "discounting." We all want and need to receive attention. We all prefer it to be positive and loving. However, a child lacking positive parental guidance quickly learns that when good attention is not available, a "discounted" form will have to do. He learns to misbehave in order to gain attention.

Let's compare this to keeping score in a game. The goal is to achieve 100 points. Good actions are worth 10; discounted are worth only 1. If there are no opportunities to score good points, then, even though it takes a lot more time and energy, the discounted tactics are implemented to score discounted points. The may not be his first choice but he remains dedicated to achieving the 100 points. Once this pattern is set, it can take a lot of work to change this programming as it becomes habitual and unconscious.

Can he ever find satisfaction through discounting?

No, although he gains points, the disapproval he receives for his negative actions robs him of the satisfaction he longs for. It would be much like trying to carry water in a holey pail. Unless this child is retrained to express a more healthy type of recognition, he will continue in this habitual pattern right into adulthood. His innate desire to find love and safety cannot be satisfied through discounting, and likely will lead to a life of repetitive difficulties that seem likely he is living in a vortex of continual negativity.

The saddest part of this situation is that the parent(s) likely operate from the same beliefs and patterning so they reinforce the child's actions with their own unhealthy choices.

Johnny loved his mom. He loved to do anything for her. Since his dad died, Johnny doesn't get much attention from his mom and none from any men. Before his life was turned upside down, he loved being at home. His mom and dad talked a lot together and spent time with him telling him stories and teaching him fun things.

One day, his mom came to the school to get him. She took him to a counsellor's office and sadly informed him that his dad had been killed that day in a car accident.

Nothing was ever the same. Johnny's mom stayed at work longer. When she came home, she hid in her room. On the rare occasion when she talked to him, it was only to scold him.

Johnny wanted to go to his mom, to hold her, to cry, to try to understand what had happened to his happy life. The more he tried, the greater the distance grew between him and his mother.

Finally, one day his mother received a phone call at work from the school principal. Johnny had become very angry with another child during a break. For no justifiable reason, he started beating the other child. Luckily, a teacher was nearby.

When asked to come to the school to discuss the matter, his mother made the excuse that it was a school problem. It was theirs to handle.

The beatings became a routine until finally, the police intervened. Johnny would now have to go to court and likely jail. Johnny was finally getting the attention he so craved.

No matter how hard a person tries to satisfy their need for attention through "discounted" actions, they just cannot find fulfilment. Even if they did receive positive influences, it would be treated as suspect because it is unfamiliar.

How often do we see situations of this nature in our newspapers? Without adequate help, a person like Johnny will have an adult life filled with traumatic events. As the desire for attention from females grows for him, He will likely engage with women who cannot give him enough attention. Even if they are with him constantly, he will still need more than they can possibly supply.

His jealousy of any contact she has with other men will evoke anger. He may even commit violence toward them … all in the name of love.

So, my friend, let's have a look at how your relationships got to be where they are today, and what one can do about them.

Before we start, I feel it is important to mention that there are always the good and the challenging aspects of any relationships anybody participates in. Even the most troubling of relationships, like in the story just mentioned, has some good things about it. And, even the healthiest relationships have challenges. Welcome to life!

We all hope that, for the most part, all of our relationships are good and healthy and that we have the tools to deal with the challenging parts. I hope what you are learning right now is helping you achieve this goal.

Let's look at some important questions that will help you define your relationship style.

Although, intimate relationships will seem to take most of the focus, the same process also can be used to explore other relationships. After all, relationships are interactions with other people, no matter whom and why they are participating.

Who do you suppose were your primary role models that influenced you?

Most likely, it was my mother and father, right?

Why? They were your essential support system when you were a child. They were the people responsible for feeding, clothing and housing you. Your whole world existed through your parents.

Who was the dominant role model for you? Was it your mom or your dad?

Interestingly enough, even if one or both parents were absent to any degree, they still influenced how you came to know relationships. Each day as we watch our parents live the moments of their lives, we learn "how it is done."

In the best case scenario, Mom and Dad married "for the right reasons" and maintained the love they felt for each other all through their lives, "until death does them part." In their love for each other, they chose to birth children, cared for them well, guided them and taught them healthy rules. They made sure the children were prepared to succeed in life. This mom and dad had plenty of time to spend with their family members; investing in each one, as a resource for the future. There were lots of healthy touching, discussions and other sharing. Life is filled with happiness.

Even in a worst-case scenario where a child lives in foster homes throughout much of his youth, with no support and no connection to the birth parents, he will still be influenced by their choices and actions. Absence is a form of action. There is a natural desire to know your birth parents. The fact that they are not available only changes the desire from knowing and growing to one of wanting, with a feeling of abandonment. Many times a child will fantasize about the absent parent, dreaming that they are "bigger than life." They become what I refer to as a "Disneyland parent." The child's belief about the parent is over-magnified. The child believes that if this parent came home, all of their needs, wants and desires would be satisfied. This belief can often cause antagonism between the child and the resident caregiver. No matter how hard this person tries to satisfy the needs of this child, he believes the absentee parent can do better.

It does not matter how the family dynamics are, there will always be a more dominant role model. The child will always lean emotionally toward one parent or caregiver over the other. This is neither good nor bad, it just is.

Please take a moment now. Look at your family and try to determine who played the part of your dominant role model? Who did you choose to fashion your personality after? Who was most important for you to get approval and attention from?

How often do we hear "Oh, you are just like your dad!" This is the dominant role model patterning. How about "Do it for your mom, okay?" In some schools of psychology, they say that we choose a variation of these four personality types:

- Just like Dad
- Just like Mom
- The opposite of Dad
- The opposite of Mom

These sound like cut and dried statements, but if you look closely, one of them will be dominant. There will be times when one of the others will fit but generally, you will fall into one of the four. Which is yours?

Is it true that if you are a boy, you will be like your dad? Or if you are a girl, you will take after your Mom?

Not at all! There will be one parent we are attracted to more than the other. I think where the modeling falls into place, is in our perception of what we believe we have to do in order to get the attention we desire from our "favourite" parent.

How often we see in parent/child relationships one of these patterns:
   a. Boys are taught to be "good boys" for their moms
   b. Girls are taught to be "the apples of daddy's eyes."

These patterns become so ingrained that many of us spend our whole lives trying to be "good boys" and "daddy's girls" in the pursuit of gaining approval from our dominant parent.

As adults, men will do almost anything to get the approval and attention of the fairer sex, from dressing the right way to working in careers that are "mother approved." Girls seek the adulation of men by the way they walk, dress, wear makeup and even talk.

Another effect in the family environment focuses on what you did, in order to receive the required amount of attention. Here are some possibilities:

- Did really well at school
- Skipped classes
- Talked louder than anyone else
- Became very quiet
- Learned to play a musical instrument
- Became a Little Suzy Homemaker
- Left messes everywhere
- Helpful with chores
- Acted lazy
- Got sick often

Note that because any of these events or perceptions became a habit, it is still part of your way of acting out your life, unless you have taken steps to change it.

Now that you are an adult, how many of these unconscious remnants are still affecting your relationships and your success in life?

Here are some examples to get your mind going.

Margie and Tom

Margie was definitely the "apple of her dad's eye." Everything she did made him very happy. She did well in school because her dad praised her for her good marks. She was a good athlete because her dad said it was important.

She never learned to cook though, because Mom was jealous of how important Margie was to her dad. Mom didn't want to teach Margie how to cook because she feared being upstaged by her daughter.

Margie never had time to clean her room because she was so busy getting her dad's approval. This angered Mom because she liked a clean house. Mom often yelled at her. Margie became more resistant to her mother's demands, which aggravated the situation even more.

Eventually, Margie grew up and married Tom. Tom loved the fact that Margie was so smart and athletic. Tom doted over his wife, praising her for her achievements. For the first couple of years, Tom tolerated a messy house because his wife was so busy with her career. Margie could not cook, so they ate out often.

Serious problems began to arise once the arrival of children required one of them to "retire" from their career. Tom wanted Margie to stay home because "it was the woman's job to raise the kids." Margie feared staying home because she would be forced to do "domestic labour."

Bob and Rosemary

Bob was a typical child. He liked his family. He really enjoyed playing with his pals. They played endlessly in the woods near his home.

The only thing he loved more than his time with the guys was finding the treat his mother had for him, when he returned home from his adventure. Sometimes, it was a special sandwich made of his favourite bread with peanut butter and creamy honey. Other times, it was lemon meringue pie. It was always something he loved.

Bob was very smart. He learned quickly that if he did what his mother wanted, there was always a reward. She often said to him, "Be a good boy and bring me...." He never thought about what he really wanted, he only thought about the reward he would receive for being a "good boy."

When he became an adult, Bob became very successful in business at a very young age. His mother was so proud of him. Her friends never tired of hearing the stories about what a wonderful boy her son was.

Soon Bob met Rosemary. It was love at first sight. Bob would do anything for Rosemary. He brought her gifts regularly. They dined out at the finest restaurants and regularly made weekend trips to the country.

Rosemary lived for the attention she received from Bob. She looked forward to the new trinket or flowers that would become hers. She loved the attention she received as she and Bob became more intimate with each other.

Everything went well; they just seemed so perfect for each other. It was no surprise when the wedding announcements arrived. Bob and Rosemary were to become husband and wife.

The honeymoon was soon over, once they moved in together. The gifts from Bob slowed to a trickle. He hardly praised her for anything since he hardly found anything in this life worthy of praise. In his eyes, Rosemary could not look after him the way his mom had. He regularly heard complaints about his working too many hours.

Rosemary quietly pulled inside of herself except to

chastise Bob for his lack of attention. She put little attention into her home. She dressed up well for work, but at home, she lounged in her housecoat from morning to night. Inside herself, she cried for the attention she had received before they married. What had gone wrong? Where was this man that she had known so many years before? Bob wondered what he had seen in this woman who no longer valued his efforts.

What about the dynamics of the relationships itself? Do we create similar relationships to those of our parents?

Can you see how each one of the characters in each of these examples patterned their relationship style after a parent? We learn all the basics about relationships from our parents. We watch our mom and dad interact over and over during our childhood. The repeated lessons become ingrained in our memories. And guess what our relationships look when we become adults?

If our mom and dad are best friends and spend lots of good times together, it is likely that you and your partner will also be best friends.

In a family where the dad is very strong and dominating while the mom is a "wallflower" submitting to his every wish, there will likely be much confusion for the children. It is likely that the sons will grow up either to be very dominating or will live in turmoil because part of him wants to dominate but another part finds treating women this way leaves him feeling angry. Daughters will either pattern after their mom or will find themselves in relationships where they dominate like their dad, as they lash out internally at their mom for not standing up for herself.

I was camping at an ocean side park with a friend a few years ago. As we were walking down the beach, we noticed an elderly couple strolling toward us. Their movements were completely synchronized. Without a word, they moved like they were welded together, and yet their only connection was the gentle touch of their hands. It was easy to see the love and high regard they had for each other. When two people become so bonded with each other, they communicate nonverbally so well, there is no need to verbalize their thoughts. Their interactions are spontaneous and unanimous. Their affinity for each other forms a strong basis for their very existence.

I have often thought of them since that time. I wonder what their children are like. With that strong of a bond, they were likely incredible parents. Lucky kids!

Jack and Theresa

Jack and Theresa had been married for over thirty years. It had been a long, tiring relationship for both of them. Not many years after they had taken their vows to love each other eternally and forsake all others, they each discovered that they did not really like the person they had chosen to spend their lives with. However, their beliefs told them that they had "chosen their bed to sleep in." Quietly, they lived in the sadness of their own solitude.

In the first five years, Theresa gave birth to four sons. They were healthy, fun loving boys. As the boys grew, they became inseparable from each other. They loved their parents, enjoying the independent attention they received. Never did the boys question the fact that their parents slept in separate rooms. Holidays seemed very normal when Mom took them to see their cousins and Dad took them camping.

As each of the boys married, they chose women just like mom. The wives looked after all their needs, the boys never having to share in the duties of home life. The boys often camped together on the weekends when they weren't playing sports or other "guy stuff."

As the children came along, each of the wives cared for them alone. They took them in the summer to see relatives. The boys enjoyed the children, taking them camping and teaching them how to play sports. It was not many years until the house was not big enough, as Mom needed her own room.

I can keep giving you examples forever, showing how children pattern their relationships after the style of their parents. Until free choice is implemented, the pattern will likely continue. Unfortunately, the path of life is not very clear for anyone, so we just keep moving through the days watching and trying to figure out how to survive the best we can with the knowledge we have.

This is why I am so keen on helping people understand the importance of being in tune with themselves. It is the only way I know of that truly allows permanent, positive change.

Where relationship patterning gets really confusing, is when children find themselves subjected to multiple sets of parents. In my own situation, my parents divorced when I was four. We lived with my father and a woman that he wed very soon after. My brother, two sisters and I lived with them until the year I was fifteen. Through very difficult circumstances, we then found ourselves living with my real mother, her second husband and our two younger half-brothers.

In this type of relationship circumstance, it is hard for a child's mind to comprehend the complexities of all the changes in parenting styles. I really found my mind spinning with all the different variables each parent represented.

Some of the questions that kept my mind busy were:
- Why did Mom go away in the first place?
- Why didn't she take me with her?
- Why did I get left with Dad?
- What did "I do" wrong to cause this?
- Who is this new woman who is trying to be mom?
- Where did Mom go?
- Why do I feel so alone?

Later on, when we were re-united with our real mom, new questions popped up:

- Is Dad going to punish us for abandoning him?

- Who is this woman who says she is my mom?

- How am I supposed to act with this woman?

- How do I do as she wishes when I have been taught differently before?

- What do I call her?

- What do I do with this new dad?

- Will he treat me better?

I realized many conflicting beliefs developed through these two segments of my life. It is difficult enough learning through one set of parents. Three sets combined, was almost incomprehensible!

Maybe this is why I have chosen to spend a lifetime coming to understand and clarify my beliefs while retraining myself as the questions about my life keep surfacing. I knew deep down inside that there had to be a more acceptable and less confusing way to live than I had come to know… and a whole lot less painful!

It was my great fortune that when I went to live with my mom, I was introduced to a man who literally changed my concept of myself, and relationships. Although my mother was not an openly affectionate person, both of my "new" parents showed me a different kind of relationship.

Upon our arrival, Mom immediately set to assessing our emotional and physical health. She made sure we got counselling, even though the family could not afford the cost. She even drove me to school everyday to a nearby town, so I could finish off the year without changing schools. (Previously, I often had changed schools more than once per year)

My Step-Dad is an amazing man. Through their marriage, Mom and Dad had birthed two of their own sons. Although both Mom and Dad worked, they could barely afford to keep the roof over their own heads. Dad could have said no when the time came for us to move in.

Dad said yes, and I got to know what a real father was like. He was a quiet man who lived every day for what it offered. He had no major aspirations for his life. He just lived to support his family. He was very devoted to Mom and all six of "their" children.

Dad was a truck driver. On weekends, I would go with him to work. All day we would drive around and hang out together. It felt so comfortable to be with him. I felt safe for the first time in my life.

For several years, we bowled together in a league. I learned how to share time with other people, rather than the old pastime of hiding in my bedroom. We spent many evenings playing board games like Scrabble. I really came to love my new family.

Because of the change-a rounds that occurred between these two sets of parents, when I became an adult, I had a great deal of confusion about the workings of relationships. Through the dynamics of each set I saw good aspects as well as bad ones. The challenge for me was recognizing and being able to do something about the beliefs that did not seem to work. Fortunately, I was blessed with a strong drive to grow.

I knew I enjoyed the close company of a female companion. I did not understand how a woman liked to be treated. I feared hurting anyone who got close, so I couldn't relax enough for either of us to feel safe. I also feared letting myself be too open, because I didn't want to get hurt either, but the need to be held and comforted kept me trying.

I knew that being disrespectful to other people was not okay. I feared being like my real father. As a result, touching another person did not feel natural, because if I were truly "like my father," I would likely hurt them. Yet, this was all I had known in my early years.

As I persevered in finding my mate, I found myself in many situations where all I knew how to do was run. In my world of relationships I felt like I was a yo-yo. I wanted to share life with another person, but not have good tools to work with; so they tended to be short-lived and filled with plenty of drama. I continually bounced from relationship to no relationship, to another relationship for many years...

Having a very curious nature, and being well aware of my lack of relationship skills, I tested out new ideas with each opportunity. It must have been very challenging for the people I shared with. As I look back over the years, I can see how the changes I have made have helped me reshape my destiny and allowed interacting with others to be easy and comfortable in almost any situation.

I realize how well I am doing now, and how much I have embraced my true spirit. There are so many wonderful people in my life that I share strong relationships with. There is even a very special lady in my life now, and we get along great! This gives me even more resolve to help others so they can let go of the pain and embrace a new more functional life style.

It is obvious that my persistence has paid off. I know the need to understand and overcome the lessons I learned as a child are the major motivators on the path I have chosen, including the writing of this book.

I knew that much of what I had learned, as a child, was wrong. I also knew I did not know what "right" looked like, but I was determined to find out.

Every relationship I have known has brought me new insight into what I believe is the basis for a functional, healthy relationship. I have spent a lifetime exploring the dynamics of being a living, breathing human being through books, seminars and personal learning, questioning every detail of my life, while coming to find peace in myself. Now, my friend, I hope you benefit from my experience.

そ

Here comes the heavy part. We are going to look at some examples of relationship situations, and try to answer these questions:

- Can people who have only known "bad" relationships, develop a healthy relationship?

- What areas of personal interaction need to be addressed in order to heal relationships?

- What can be done differently to establish better interactions?

Let's think of some examples of, let's call them relationship malfunctions to get some thinking going. There may be more than we can come up with, but at least they will get you thinking.

Remember, the bases of any of these issues were learned in childhood. Please be aware that familiarity provides a level of comfort that entices us to stay the same as before, so if we want to make big changes, we need to be willing to make different choices to get us out of that old comfort zone.

One more thing, the focus of this section is intended for your personal growth alone. The desired outcome here is for you to understand how you perform in interactions with others. It is about your stuff. The work you do is meant to benefit you. It is not about blaming the other person or finding ways to make them change.

The only person you can ever change is yourself.

Just as a precursor, I feel that I need to remind you that you may not like some of the answers. That is okay. This is not about agreeing with me, it is, as I said before about looking into your own way of getting through your life so you can decide what needs to change. Remember, there is always help available if you feel stuck.

**I can't say it enough times;
it truly is all about you!**

Here are a few examples of real life situations that may help you understand what I am trying to get at. See if you can pick situations from your own life and try to figure out your causes. It is fun if you don't take yourself too seriously.

1.The problem:

My spouse is very controlling. I can't do anything without their approval. I am even checked for how long I take to get home from work. What is my current emotional benefit in this relationship?

Controlling spouses indicate a lack of willingness for you to take dominion for yourself, a sense of powerlessness. There are belief systems in play that indicate that you believe you are not capable of looking after yourself at an emotional level.

Without having someone to run your life for you, you would have to take responsibility for yourself and your actions.

What can I do to change the situation for the better?

Start making some decisions. Make small ones first. They might be something like what to have for dinner. If your spouse tries to control your actions, lovingly tell them that you are teaching yourself to be more assertive and that you need to do this for yourself.

What do you want your life to look like? What could you do to increase your own personal power in your life based on honouring yourself?

It is important for you to learn to "recognize" situations where you are letting yourself be controlled. Ask yourself what benefit you are gaining and how you feel emotionally. Learn to check in with yourself. Ask yourself how you would really like to handle this moment and what outcome you would prefer. If you can retrain yourself to be "not" controlled, then you won't be.

2. The problem:

My spouse seems to be constantly touching (hugging, kissing, holding) me, and needing reassurance. This has been a consistent pattern for years. What is my current emotional benefit in this relationship?

It is likely that you need to feel powerful because of an unconscious belief that you have lost your power. Your spouse's perceived weakness helps you feel strong. This is commonly referred to as "care giver" syndrome. Emotionally needy people need weaker people to help them feel strong.

What can I do to change the situation for the better?

Ask yourself why you do not want to be touched. Has something happened to cause you to pull back from spouse? Your spouse may be reacting in fear to your pulling back. Not wanting to lose you, they may be overcompensating.

Another suggestion might be to determine the quality of attention you give to your spouse. If you find that you are holding back for some reason, you might look at your beliefs about touching. Could there also be any unresolved issues that you are "barricading" yourself from? Being honest with yourself and your spouse about your concerns is essential for a healthy relationship. If you can accept sharing with your partner that includes healthy touching, communication and support, the over balance will soon settle down.

3. The problem:

My spouse is a workaholic, always running between two or three jobs, bringing home a good income with each one, but always keeps excessively busy. What is my current emotional benefit in this relationship?

This is much like being safe in a non-relationship. The basic needs of food, clothing and shelter are being met. Emotionally, there is no availability for interaction. Although the relationship may seem dry and boring, it surely is emotionally safe.

What can I do to change the situation for the better?

Check out your emotional situation. Do you really want to have more emotional fulfilment in your life? Do you fear having unpleasant encounters with your spouse? Do you feel that your spouse fears having uncomfortable interactions with you? Unfortunately, in order to have the great and enjoyable feelings, you will have to face the uncomfortable ones as well. (With the bad ones you learn to appreciate the good.)

If you do want to improve your emotional quality, start by allowing yourself to feel more. What do you find pleasant? Let yourself enjoy it. Make your home more inviting for sensual expression, by including emotion-provoking articles such as pets, flowers and books. Talk about how things feel for you in a positive way to your spouse (when you get a chance to see them) or even more fun; send them a card expressing how much you love them. Be gentle, positive and provocative without expecting anything back.

An absolutely vital point for you is to learn how to gently communicate with your spouse, so you can find out what needs to be addressed. A strong sense of warmth and safety will make them want to be home more.

4. The problem:

My spouse regularly speaks in a sarcastic, condescending tone to me. What is my current emotional benefit in this relationship?

Similar to the first example, there is an underlying feeling of powerlessness. Being in a relationship with someone who overpowers you supports this belief. It also proves a belief that life is an unhappy place, and that you do not deserve any better.

What can I do to change the situation for the better?

Recognize how you let yourself be undermined by your spouse's actions. Get to know how it feels when you "are being put down." Hold yourself up tall and do not join in the game. When you are feeling put down, remind yourself that you are no longer a child.

Kindly, tell your spouse that you no longer accept being treated in this manner, and that you deserve to be treated with dignity. It is important for you to state that you love and cherish them, and you will only continue this conversation as long as the tone is respectful.

Remember that people who act in a condescending way do not feel safe. Rarely do people who communicate sarcastically ever intend to direct their venom at any particular person, including you. It is just a safety mechanism.

QTIP-Quit Taking It Personally!

Instilling true safety for both of you is vital to making long-term change.

This is a good example of how protective safety does not work in the long run.

5. The Problem:

My spouse is a total "neat freak," always after me to clean up. Dishes always have to be done right away. We rarely have any fun at home-it might mess it up! What is my current emotional benefit in this relationship?

Highly charged actions, referred clinically as obsessive compulsive, prevent people from feeling what is going on inside themselves emotionally. The situation is one continual stream of stress.

Your gain in keeping the situation distressed, is that it allows you unconsciously to feel victimized. Not having to address your own feelings of inadequacy, you have someone else to blame for the situation in your life. It's out of your control. You spend so much time resisting the situation; you have no time to look inside.

What can I do to change the situation for the better?

Recognize your own victim energy. Try to understand the value you gain from the current situation. Choose to live a healthier emotional lifestyle. Take the time to de-stress yourself, so you can stop yourself from engaging in unhealthy interactions. See the situation for what it really is... two people not feeling safe.

Teach yourself to be assertive by setting goals for yourself, and striving to attain them. Start with easy short-term goals, so you can succeed easily. This will retrain your mind to accept positive outcomes. Value your life.

What hobbies have you been denying yourself, especially ones that get you out of the house? What can you do to encourage your spouse to find fulfilment?

Another important point is to try to be objective in the situation. Is the neatness your spouse desires, really excessive? We all have differing requirements for cleanliness. By communicating effectively, there may be a compromise.

6. The Problem:

My spouse is very overweight. Spouse was quite thin when we first married but now eats "continually." What is my current emotional benefit in this relationship?

There is safety in being with someone who believes no one else wants them. This person is not likely to run away from you, nor will you have challenging encounters with them because they are burying their feelings in their body.

What can I do to change the situation for the better?

If your spouse seems emotionally unavailable and is compensating by overeating, it is likely you also have buried your emotions and feelings. You will need to find that inner strength to be the strong one in your family. Two emotionally weak people cannot support each other. However, one strong person can help the other just by being emotionally available and intimate with them through expressing your positive feelings for them. Be pleasantly encouraging. Safety is the key for both of you.

7. The Problem:

My spouse is always nagging and complaining about something. It never ends. Anything from the neighbours, the kids, the dog, work. It is very irritating. What is my current emotional benefit in this relationship?

Excessive actions like nagging are used as a barrier to keep others out. As long as the complaining continues, you do not have to try to get close to this person. It is a great method of having a "non-relationship." As long as the barrier remains, there is no exposure to vulnerability or intimacy. You are therefore, safe. You don't have to risk getting close. This situation works for you.

There may also be an underlying feeling of frustration and boredom with life. Complaining is a discounted method of getting attention.

What can I do to change the situation for the better?

Learn to stand up tall. Get past your own feelings of powerlessness. You will have to implement a take-charge attitude, with lots of love. As you become stronger, and take action in your own life work, you will create an example for others to follow. By developing a progressive atmosphere, more energy will be focused into positive forward-moving situations and less into complaining.

When the complaining starts, diffuse the conversation by turning the complaint into a positive conversation. Spouse is likely very frustrated with life, so take charge with an understanding heart. And remember to take time to play.

8. The Problem:

My spouse has quit doing anything other than drinking beer and watching television. It used to be playing ball, going for walks and romantic dinners. Now it is television sports and the evening news. What is my current emotional benefit in this relationship?

Comfort and predictability. No surprises. You are safe. There is no need to concern yourself about vulnerability or emotional risk, because a couple of beers and television and your spouse is safely tucked away for the night.

What can I do to change the situation for the better?

Action is the key here. You once enjoyed having an exciting, active life. What do you want to do with your life now? Make plans and take action. Remember to always do it with love. Making your life of value to you, by creating importance and worth in it, is a form of self-love. Showing that you can take action for yourself, will cause healthy changes and result in a better life.

9. The Problem

My spouse has an enormous wardrobe. There is no room for my clothes in any of the drawers or closets, but more clothes keeps showing up. What is my current emotional benefit in this relationship?

People who have the need for excessively elaborate wardrobes do not feel good about themselves. Something has happened in their past that has caused them to develop a belief that they are emotionally starved. They mask their feelings by "prettying" themselves up. New things mean they can leave the "old things behind." The constant flow of new clothes attempts to satisfy the emptiness through instant gratification.

Your gain is that you can avoid the past as well. Likely you will be so busy working, trying to pay the bills for all the new stuff that you don't leave time to deal with your own past hurts. Another great emotional avoidance technique.

What can I do to change the situation for the better?

The fact that your spouse feels emotionally starved, means you are not "feeding them" to their level of desired satisfaction. Dig in and find out how you feel about yourself. If you find that there is an emptiness inside, you may recognize that you are not in touch with your own emotional side. Exercises such as journaling, art therapy, music therapy and dance will help you to build a connection with yourself. As you come to realize that you are worthy of love, you will begin to sparkle. It is essential that as you come to be in touch with yourself, you will need to communicate those feelings more. Bring yourself out of the inner cave.

Life is safe and beautiful.

I hope that you recognize these examples as tools for opening the door to your own emotional make up. If they ruffled your feathers a bit, have a look in yourself and try to use the feelings emerging as a springboard for learning, rather than a reason to shut down. You may be feeling a little vulnerable right now. Be okay with it. Take a chance.

You will notice that none of the examples above related to insurmountable situations. In reality, there is no situation in life that cannot be changed for the better. All it takes is an attitude adjustment and a willingness to make the change. Getting the wild imagination (powered by fear) out of the way is essential.

Another aspect of each answer, you will notice, is that the changes implied to improve your life, only refer to actions you can take. They never imply what your spouse might need to do. Your spouse will need to do his or her own work.

Early in this session, Eva asked the question, "Why do we want to be in relationships?" At this time, I would like to re-answer that question.

Neale Donald Walsh, in his book, Conversations With God, Volume 1 explains that modern day relationships serve a totally different purpose than those of past generations. Because we no longer have serious concerns about basic survival, the dynamics of relationships have changed. Healthy, functional relationships today serve the purpose of mirroring. We have evolved to a point, where the human mass consciousness needs to mature and expand. In order to grow, we need to let go of old beliefs and limitations, particularly those based in fear. Every relationship we participate in, no matter how minimal acts as our "mirrors." They help us see how we get through life. Whatever is occurring in the lives of others you share the journey with is a mirror of what is going on in our life, emotionally. Each interaction holds a key to understanding your own life better.

If you are not happy with some aspect of your spouse's actions, please use it as an opportunity to springboard your own personal growth. There is no room for blaming your spouse for your discontentment.

Later on, we will have a session about healthy relationships; we will expand on this more at that time.

By the way, please, please listen to the thoughts in your head and the feelings in your body. If the situation is more than you believe you can handle,

get professional help. Getting professional help is a positive choice. It does not mean you should be ashamed because you are not perfect. We all have imperfections.

If there are situations where one of you is reacting to life in any manner that may be considered excessive or hazardous, do what you have to do to ensure safety for all. There is no room here for heroes or martyrs.

Three questions were asked before this exercise. How about if you re-ask them and we will see if we can answer them now, one at a time.

Can people who have only known bad relationships, develop a healthy relationship?

Yes, it is completely up to the person involved. How much do they want to have a healthy relationship? Anyone who is willing to do the work... to be honest and vulnerable with themselves will develop healthier relationships. Every time a conscious choice is made and integrated, a healthier interaction with another is possible. The more conscious and pro-active we are in making life choices, the healthier our relationships will be.

What areas of personal interaction need to be addressed in order to heal relationships?

Our purpose in this life is to find and express our wholeness as individuals. Relationships act as mirrors so we can see how we are doing our lives so we can live more effectively.

We need to address any area of our lives where we feel less than we would prefer. This is a lifetime project. It requires choosing individual aspects, which leave us feeling unsatisfied or unhappy, and then actively pursuing a new, more acceptable outcome. Choose easy ones first that are not threatening to you, or your partner. This could be possibly, determining why you don't like to help with housework, or why it is so important to have the toilet seat left in the up position. This will make it easy for your mind to accept change more readily. If you choose difficult or deep-rooted beliefs too early, you may sabotage your efforts.

Remember: When the going gets tough, the tough get help.

In fact, I would suggest that even before you get started; find a professional counsellor that you are comfortable with. This will provide you with the safety of knowing that if you do get into a bind, you have someone to reach out to. This is not an excuse to procrastinate, it is a safety measure. We are working to find more peace, joy and happiness in our lives. Please do not treat changing your life as a military action. Do it with love. You deserve the best.

What can be done differently to establish better interactions?

Hopefully, both people involved are willing to make and accept change. And hopefully, both of you can accept this new process as a medium for self-discovery. Use the information provided in Chapter One about understanding and establishing safety for both of you, before proceeding. Try to think about what end result will be the best for all, including yourself, before you start making any changes, so that you have a target to aim for.

Learn to stand back, before you make any decisions. Resolve to make no decisions that give you advantage over another. Making healthy decisions for yourself cannot cause harm to others.

When you make decisions that are good for you without undermining the power of the other, you provide an opportunity for both of you to grow. By being truly supportive of the other person as well, they can feel safe and comfortable in working their own process.

Absolutely essential during the process of healing a relationship and any other aspect of life, is communication. People are sensitive characters, often with relatively "thin skin." Being able to give and take in conversation appropriately is an essential skill. Without adequate communication skills, both verbally and emotionally, one cannot hope to achieve any kind of true satisfaction. Take the time and the interest to learn how to converse with your partner. We all speak and listen through our emotional filters. What you say is not necessarily what the other hears. Only by being able to speak the same language in conjunction with a common desire to share honestly, can people hope to effectively cooperate with each other.

If you have to do this work alone, resolve to do what is best overall for you and everyone else. This means making a progressive choice that will truly empower you to be a more functional person. The mere fact that your partner is interacting with you as you go through any changes will cause them to change as well.

It's a rule of life, that nothing can remain static while amidst chaos. As you create change, you create chaos.

Because you have changed, it affects everyone around you.

The others in your life are forced into chaos and will have to make changes, whether they want to or not.

There are only three results that can be derived from implementing conscious change while interacting with someone who is acting resistant to change.

1. Nothing will happen and life will appear to "carry on" as always.
2. Others will respond to your efforts and start to change as well.
3. Relationships will end, as you discover you are not on the same wavelength. You no longer serve purpose in each others life.

Any of these results is fine with the rest of us. However, you have to live with yourself and your choices. You must choose what works for you as an individual in the long term. Just walk slowly, cautiously and respectfully and things will always work out for the best.

It is my belief, and the intention of this book, to help each of us to maintain and improve any of the relationships we are currently having. It is so much easier to heal inside existing partnerships, than to create more upheaval in our lives by "throwing out" what may be a perfectly good relationship that just needs some work. Divorce and separation are just too costly at any level. To quit trying without truly knowing that the relationship has nothing left to offer defeats the true purpose of the connection. A new relationship will only take up where the old one left off, unless some kind of intervention occurs that causes profound change.

Be patient. Be gentle with yourself and your partner.
Do not expect instant results.
Learn to recognize your feelings of fear.
Base any decisions on love.

Please reflect on the section of the previous chapter that discusses personal responsibility. It is so vitally important for you to understand and accept that the choices others around you make, as a result of your chaos, are theirs to own.

If you are doing what you truly believe is best, things will always work out for the best. So how about those healthy relationships before we wrap up for today?

Sounds good, so first of all let's define what a healthy relationship is.

A healthy relationship is an interaction between two people who respect each other as individuals. They recognize that everyone has strengths and challenges. In a healthy relationship, there is no power play. Each person supports the other person in the evolution to his or her own personal enlightenment. Each person is self-responsible and supports the other person to be the same. Each participant promotes honesty, integrity and safety for all.

Do people who have developed healthy relationships still have challenging beliefs systems?

As long as we are on this planet, we will have issues to work on. It is part of evolving, the peeling of the onion, so to speak. The difference between a healthy relationship and one that is not is the level of personal awareness and self responsibility. One must be mindful or conscious of their participation in life in order to attract and maintain a functional, healthy relationship.

As a dysfunctional belief expresses itself, a conscious person becomes aware of it, owns it and does something about it. The other person supports them in doing so.

Each person in this relationship stands by their partner in total commitment. They provide support by allowing them the conditions they need, so they can expose and release the belief in order to embrace a new outcome.

Do people in healthy relationships have difficult times?

Yes, but the main difference is that the participants do not capitalize on the other person's vulnerability. Each person strives to assist the other to be as strong as possible and support them in times of weakness.

Healthy people accept and rejoice in their strengths and weaknesses and provide the room and support to allow their partner to do the same. They see themselves and their partner as a human being and a work in progress. They manage "less than healthy" situations and turn them into healthy interactions.

Healthy people live healthier lives. They are happier, more successful and content knowing that their world is safe and good. Life becomes much easier and more joyful.

Healthy people attract other healthy people into their lives. It always boils down to the point that our external life is a mirror of what is going on inside of us. If we like what is going on, we can keep it. If we don't like what is going on, we can change.

It is all a matter of choice.

What Mom and Dad Didn't Know They Were Teaching You

This is one of the most important chapters in this book, not to make light of the information provided in the other discourses. I feel that when we have a clear understanding of what went on when we were children, we will be in a position to make more informed decisions affecting any choices in our current circumstances.

In this chapter we will explore some examples relating to how our parents lived and taught us unconsciously. We will learn how to understand, *What Mom and Dad Didn't Know They Were Teaching You.*

What can there be that Mom and Dad didn't know? Aren't grown ups supposed to be completely aware of what they are doing?

Here's an example of what I am trying to get across.

Envision a young child sitting in the family room playing with his Game Boy. While he is totally engrossed in his entertainment, his mom and dad are having a heated discussion because mom didn't remember to pick up ketchup while she was at the grocery store.

He hears, "How can you be so stupid? You don't work, all you have to do is look after the house, and yet you can't remember something as simple as ketchup!"

As the discussion continues, the "conversation" his parents are creating, erodes into a full-scale battle. In the middle of this interchange, big sister enters the room seeking money so she can go to the movies with her friends.

By now, his dad has had enough and yells at her, "Do you people realize that I have to work very hard every day to keep this family going? Do you realize it is me who puts the food on the table around here?" And so on.

What impact do you think this situation had on this young boy, as he played nearby?

He may not have actively participated, but he still learned from it. We are like sponges. When there is an opportunity to learn, we do it, and we do it well. As I have said before, our mind does not care whether the information is meant for us or whether it is even the truth. In this case, this young lad learned a lot. How often do situations of this nature occur in every child's life?

I can certainly understand what the young lad learned. I can also appreciate how Mom and Dad didn't know that they were even teaching them to him.

In this case, it is clearly defined by the parents' interactions that "men are superior to women," "being a stay at home Mom is not a worthwhile or meaningful occupation" and "dad is king of the house because he is the breadwinner." These are very common examples of core beliefs that develop unintentionally while life goes on, and have a strong impact on the realities that children adopt, even though they were not intended or even directed at the child.

We all have lived through many experiences like this one. Through the process in this chapter, we can gain a better understanding of how we came to own our beliefs.

Sounds intriguing, can we explore some of these unconscious lessons? They sure seem to get in everywhere don't they!

Depending on how we have learned the rules of life, even as adults, our mind will always seek out information to justify its beliefs …until we choose to take control and make alternative choices that produce new outcomes. The egoic mind does not care about truth; it only cares about what it "knows."

Most of the learning we accepted during our formative years was provided to us without anyone even having a clue about what was happening. We watched, listened and learned each time somebody we trusted, acted out his or her life before us.

Kind of reminds me of that piece of the poem Shakespeare wrote: The Seven Ages Of Man.

All the world's a stage,

And all the men and women merely players:

They have their exits and their entrances;

And one man in his time plays many parts,

Even back in the days of old, folks recognized that we played roles in each other's lives. Without any particular intention or desire to impart knowledge, the people around us taught us the rules that we have used until today. They went along their merry ways living life the best they knew how, with no thought to the impact they could be having on anyone else. Until recently, it was not understood how much impact we have on each other as we make the decisions that direct our life path. Each decision we make has a domino effect on our own lives, and on those of every other person we interact with.

Prior to the 1940's, virtually no information was readily available about personal growth or childrearing. There was no source where a person could turn to, in order to answer the questions of life. This changed when a new era of consciousness was ushered in, as groundbreaking information became available to parents, through a book by Dr. Benjamin Spock. *The Common Sense Book of Baby and Child Care,* (1946) taught us "everything" we needed for raising our children correctly.

Yes, I remember having my Dr. Spock book handy when my kids were little, even in the '70s. Spock was considered the "Father of Permissiveness" because he had the audacity to speak the unspeakable. He praised us for treating our children as individuals, taking the time to get to know their needs for feeling safe and loved. What amazing thinking!

Even this early literature didn't really recognize the importance of knowing that children mirror the thoughts and actions of their parents. Our parents taught us in the same manner as their parents enlightened them. There was "little" conscious decision making required to bring us to maturity. Mom and Dad responded to life the same way they had learned. They didn't have the time, skill or knowledge that they should help us to create a conscious destiny. They lived life and we reacted to it. No one ever told them that their choices shaped our view of the world.

It is claimed that over 80% of our learning is assimilated unconsciously. All the reading and experimenting we have done throughout our lives has really had minimal impact compared to the information we absorb by watching others.

Where do we learn most of our lessons from?

The most effective communication methods have little to do with speaking. Body language through facial expressions, gesturing, moving, interacting with others and tones of voice give us continual information and feedback about our world. Nothing had to be said for us to learn. And boy, do we learn!

As I have stated before, Mom and Dad were our primary teachers. As they lived their lives, we learned. If you look at your life presently, how many of the actions you make automatically and beliefs that shape your life are just repetitions echoing one of your parents?

Our parents likely had no inkling about what they were doing. In fact, they probably didn't even know they didn't know. They tried their best and likely put great thought into raising us, but without a proper understanding of what children really need to learn in order to get the most out of their lives, how could they possibly know they were having such a profound effect on our psyches?

It's frustrating to see that things have changed very little though isn't it? How many times did I tell myself I never want to be like my mom, and yet so often I see her through my actions!

You're right. Even today, many young people thrust themselves into parenthood with no clue about the huge responsibility they have taken on. They so often have no idea what is entailed in molding the lives of their offspring...and so the cycle continues.

All they seem to see is that a baby is a means to get the love they desperately desire from an uninterruptible source. However, not all is lost. More and more information is becoming available about new personal growth techniques. All we have to do now is help people generally, to realize that:

Life is a matter of choice, not habit.
Those choices always have consequences.
Good choices make good consequences.

Being that the rules of life are not always clearly visible, we have to come to a level of awareness that helps us to realize that something is "wrong with our program." Once we make the choice to participate in our own evolution, we need to find some starting points and begin to consciously fix things so that our process of healing can be expedited.

Sounds like a daunting task, where do we start?

Remember, life is lived one breath at a time. Therefore, one thought at a time, too. One of the best places to start the search, for the beliefs we learned as children, is by learning how to recognizing our ingrained thinking patterns. Let's start with some commonly stated beliefs that have often occurred through the years, divide them up into different arenas and have a look at what we have done to ourselves. How many of these do you recognize? You can probably add many more once you see the patterning in your own life. We all have lots of them.

Can you name me some?

The difference between being boys and girls.

- Girls do the dishes and learn to cook while the boys learn to work on cars
- A woman has to be a good cook and homemaker to be of any value
- A man's role is to make money, not keep house
- Boys can stay out later at night than girls

- Boys can wrestle (defend themselves) but girls are too delicate
- Boys are smarter than girls
- Girls should not bother getting an education as they are just going to get married anyway
- If girls did get an education it was likely to become a secretary, nurse or teacher.
- Boys could be anything they wanted but if they wanted to be "successful" they should become doctors or lawyers
- Boys can get wild and have sex early while girls should stay virgins until they marry.

And this is what we learned form them.

- Men need a woman to look after them
- A woman's place is at home looking after her man
- Women are inadequate if they can't cook or keep house
- Men are inadequate if they don't make huge incomes
- It's better to be a male than a female
- Girls are "less than" boys
- Men are smarter
- Even if women are "smart," they should not show it
- Having sexual needs is only for men

How about some more? What about relationships?

- Yelling is the most effective way of being heard
- He who talks the loudest gets heard
- Being drunk justifies hitting your spouse
- Being angry is justification for being abusive
- Dad is boss because he is biggest
- A woman's place is in the home looking after her man
- It is okay for men to display sexuality, but not for women
- Affection should never be displayed in front of the children
- Do what I say, not what I do

And your interpretation?

Speaking your mind is not a safe thing to do

- Considering other people's feelings is not important
- Physical violence is okay
- Alcohol justifies any actions taken
- Big people or men are to be feared because they are stronger
- Normal bodily feelings including sexuality are bad and should be overcome
- Positive touching and showing affection are wrong
- It's not acceptable to express feelings, good or bad
- I have to justify how I feel, so therefore I cannot let myself be natural with my feelings

You're good! How about money?

- Mom and Dad's needs come first
- Money doesn't grow on trees
- Rich people deserve more respect than "regular" people
- Being rich is everything
- There's never enough
- If you work hard enough you will have everything you want
- He who has the most toys at the end wins

Right on! Can you see the relationship?
- Satisfying addictions is more important than healthy needs
- There is not enough money for everyone
- Money determines a person's value and position in life
- People who are not motivated by money are unsuccessful and misdirected
- Large quantities of money cannot be made honestly or without hard work
- Having is more important than being

And one that was very scary to me as a child, punishment.

- Dad metes out the punishment (just wait till your father comes home)
- Go to your room and stay there until I tell you to come out
- Go to bed without supper
- Hitting is okay to bring children in line
- Taking away food from a child is "effective punishment"
- If you want to cry, I will give you something to cry about!
- I will wash your mouth out with soap.

We sure learn a lot when we are kids, don't we?

- Men are superior
- Women are more delicate than men
- Bedrooms are where bad people get sent
- People who make mistakes do not deserve to have
- I only get to keep things if I am good
- It is acceptable for my care givers to hit me
- Because I am small, I do not deserve respect
- Expression of emotions such as crying is wrong, and punishable
- Acts of violence or abuse are justifiable when meted out as deterrents

And one last one, who is boss?

- Parents are to feared
- Control is gained by being loud
- Do what I say, not what I do
- There is a price to pay for being an individual
- If you are bad, the police will come and take you away
- God will punish you if you are bad
- Eat everything that is put in front of you

It never ceases to amaze me how many people are disempowered by this factor: authority. What have you got for this one?

- You have to be big to be powerful
- Small people can not be powerful
- Loud people are scary
- Other people are more powerful than we are
- People who are supposed to protect me, hurt me
- Making mistakes is bad and punishable
- I will get hurt if I express my individuality
- Don't listen to my body
- Authority figures (parents) know best and should never be questioned
- Educated people know best
- God only loves people who are good
- Fear authority figures
- It is not safe to be me

Isn't it amazing the long list of beliefs that are available to us through being silent witnesses?

It's almost unending!

We have a myriad of beliefs that our parents have taught us; it's a fact of life. How many of them are active in your life?

So now that we are aware of these belief statements, what can we do about them?

Take the time to listen closely to yourself. Every person processes thousands of thoughts daily. How many of them do we really listen to? How many do we really understand? What are you telling yourself?

Witness consciousness is the key to awareness. Allow yourself to go within, not as an escape, but as a vehicle for accessing total power and self-knowledge. It gives you the ability to know what drives you. It takes courage to stand back and let your thoughts surface. Some of those thoughts likely have scary memories that some part of you wants to avoid. All you need to do is remember that they are just thoughts, and have no power over you. The ability to detach from your thoughts and memories will come easily assisting you in diffusing them. This would be a good time to review chapter one on Safety, just as a refresher.

Most importantly, remember:

With detachment comes enlightenment

Every thought has a story inside it, an experience from that injured child that you have protected all your life. What is your story? How do you protect yourself? What are you really protecting yourself from? Are you ready to look at your story? Are you ready to do something about it? Can you stand back and look at your story without becoming protective? By taking the time to be still, you can allow yourself to hear what your mind is really trying to tell you. Remember; find your inner strength first.

One helpful change that can be made is to turn off the radio. So many people today cannot seem to bear the silence. However, one cannot listen to what is going on in their head, when an external noise is running rampant over their thoughts, blocking out any internal messages. How will they ever find true peace when they continually create a battle between their mind and their ears?

Like anything else in life, excess is not good for us. We need to have time for pleasure, but it must not be used as an escape from what our mind is attempting to tell us.

If you feel fear when you think of allowing yourself into your head, then that is your first belief to recognize. What a great place to start! It will be very difficult to hear any of your thoughts if you cannot quiet your world enough to hear beyond the noise.

Why is it so important to listen to the noise in my head? I would rather just tune it out.

If we are going to make any impact on our well-being, we must take the time to listen. The noise will only get louder, the longer we avoid listening to it. I believe that avoidance of the constant call for attention from our mind is one of the leading causes of unhappiness and stress in life. We train ourselves to tune out rather than tuning in.

The result is that our mind has to expend more effort to get our attention. If we do not listen to that first call, the stakes are increased until we can no longer avoid the situation. This is the cause of many of the challenging situations that occur in our lives including difficult relationships, accidents, illness and general unhappiness. Our higher mind just wants to be heard.

How many times as children did we watch our mentors do what ever they could to prevent hearing themselves? Excessive actions such as burying one's self into television night after night, having to have the radio on all the time, drinking alcohol excessively and overworking occur as a result of the drive to avoid facing those unbearable thoughts.

As adults, how many forms of escape do we use? How do we justify them? How many times have you heard someone say that they need to do some "habit" because they are afraid of the thoughts in their head? They go stir crazy if they do not keep themselves busy.

Are there safety issues that need to be dealt with?

Yes. When one feels they need to avoid listening to

their own thoughts, there has to be a reason. It would likely be that some of those thoughts leave them feeling unsafe.

Recognizing that safety is an issue is vital.
Establishing safety is mandatory.

One cannot explore the voices in their heads while feeling that they might be hurt by what they might hear.

Is there more to it than just standing back and being detached?

Believe it or not, that is the secret to getting past those thoughts. Any thought we pay attention to, or even more importantly, identify with, will strengthen from the power we give it. By detaching from the thought, once we have calmed down enough, we can view it like watching a movie. Then we can see more clearly what the thought is actually telling us. Once the message is clear, we have no more need for the thought, so we detach and let it pass. Eventually, it will weaken and then cease to express, because it is not being fed.

This does not mean avoidance from
dealing with the fear!

What's an example of interpreting a thought so I might get the message from it?

John really likes Melissa. He thinks about her all day. He dreams of the day they will marry and spend the rest of their life on easy street. Unfortunately, Melissa does not feel quite the same. She likes John a lot, but does not want to engage with him in an intimate relationship. John keeps pressing Melissa for more time together.

Melissa has quite recently left a difficult relationship. She feels fearful about letting anyone get close. In her past encounters with men, she has been the one who got hurt. John keeps trying to hug her, but she keeps pushing him away. Inside, she wants to let him be close and protect her, but she automatically resists when he comes near. Melissa is aware that she is running from yet another relationship. Melissa doesn't know what to do.

In John's mind, his obsession with Melissa keeps him busy. He goes from thoughts of the ecstasy of touching her to anger over her constant rejection of his advances. The intensity of his thoughts keeps him from recognizing that she is not willing to start an intimate relationship. The excessive consumption of thinking energy keeps him away from recognizing that he feels inadequate and unloved. Instead of than trying to fill his need externally, it would be best for him to stand back and see for himself how he tries to have other people "fill his hole." Once he recognizes that he needs to find ways to access his own inner fulfilment, he will be better equipped for any relationships.

Since Melissa attracted this kind of an interaction into her life, she likely needs to address the same issues of neediness. The difference for her would be the need to determine why she sets up blocks to prevent any kind of closeness. It would be necessary for her to have a look at her needs for keeping people out of her life. Standing back would allow her to see how and why she does her blocking process. She could then start to recognize her own fears, and understand how they originated (core beliefs). Melissa will gradually retrain herself to feeling and expressing her own beautiful, loving nature.

Taking a less pressured approach in their relationship would be helpful for both. Becoming friends, if they can, first will allow them the safety and space to deal with their issues before the pressures of premature intimacy derail their respective chances for growth. John and Melissa both need space and support.

What could they do once they recognize the actual message?

If both John and Melissa were willing, the most exponential growth for them, as individuals, would come from joint counselling sessions. Working together, they would be able to more readily see how their actions affect other people, while keeping themselves from receiving what they truly want; a healthy, satisfying relationship.

During their own introspection, they will come to recognize how they have patterned their relationship process after the way their parents interacted. By recognizing the unconscious training, they can choose to participate more effectively.

When Melissa realizes that her mom barricaded herself

emotionally from her dad and she followed suit, she can consciously choose to learn to risk letting people she feels safe with, into her life. She will learn that John's pattern emulates the actions of her dad. By making conscious choices, she will no longer attract men who overwhelm her and she will feel better about intimacy.

John recognizes that his parents never took the time to enhance their relationship by sharing time together. Both parents were too busy working. When John's dad wanted attention from his wife, she either had household chores to do or was too tired. John saw that his dad got the attention he desired by constantly being in her space, trying to draw her affections.

By taking the time to work together, John and Melissa can recognize and undo the old patterning. The eventual outcome will be that neither one will attract someone who triggers the old patterns, nor any thoughts that suggest life is not safe. John and Melissa might choose at the end of the counselling sessions to not engage in a relationship together, but they will each be in a healthier position to attract a more suitable mate. The choice to live a healthier life style is a positive gain for both of them. Staying detached from the outcome is necessary. There is no risk if both people feel safe while having no expectations.

Being able to find their real selves, by breaking free of the old learned patterns enhances the quality of their lives. The less people have to invest in fending off undesirable thoughts, the more energy can be invested in creating and living in better health mentally, physically, emotionally and spiritually. Freedom from old limiting beliefs allows the energy inside the body to flow more easily, promoting more rapid healing and personal evolution.

What greater benefit can be gained by any action in our life, than by taking the time to listen quietly to ourselves? By discovering the truth behind our thoughts, we can let go resulting in a much less intense lifestyle. We would not have to work to keep up the barriers we protect ourselves with. We could now be more receptive to new opportunities that offer better health, more happiness and greater success. When we quit running away from ourselves and recreate our path, life becomes easier. By working in congruence with ourselves, we, in effect, become our own best friends.

**Who in this life would make a better best friend
to each of us than ourselves?**

By recognizing that our old rules are our own creations, we can more easily understand, *What Mom and Dad Didn't Know They Were Teaching You.*

There is no one in the way of our evolution but us!

It is absolutely essential for each of us to remember that we created our own belief system. We cannot blame others for how our life goes. Mom and Dad are not to be held at fault. We created our beliefs though our own perceptions. It can only follow then, that if we created them, we can change them. What is that old adage?

If it is to be, it is up to me!

The Healing Process

What is the point to all this concern about looking into our pasts? Why can't I just leave well enough alone?

Leaving things alone has brought you to where you are today. The questions I return to you are,

- Do you want to keep living your life the way it is now?

- Is it better for you to keep running your life with little protection or control over circumstances,

- Would it be better for you to make some conscious choices that help you make sense of your life and make it work better?

Living is much like flying an airplane. It is helpful to plan your destination, before you take off. If you don't have a destination in mind, you will burn a lot of extra fuel while you are deciding where to land. If you don't make a conscious landing point, you will keep ending up in places you might not want to be.

Narrowing down the choices for your landing is the main reason for not leaving well enough alone.

You might not clearly know where you ultimately want to land but if you have a general idea at least, you can hone the landing information as you move closer to it. Learning to feel your way through life, listening to your inner voice will guide you better than any other method available. Your highest consciousness knows our best destination. All you have to do is get clear and trust the process.

Remember
Our ultimate goal is to land where we choose
Not where life throws us!

If living life unconsciously was good enough for our ancestors, why is it not good enough for us?

If you take a moment to think about what life looked like when you were a child, you can see an unbelievable number of changes that have occurred. Whether you are twenty or seventy years of age, many aspects of life have changed so dramatically that it hardly looks like this is still the same lifetime.

I remember a friend of mine telling the story about her grandparents when they arrived from Sweden around the early 1900's. Could you put yourself in their place? They arrived to their new home, about one hundred miles north of Edmonton, Alberta, Canada in the late spring. Their dream home, when they arrived, was a piece of boreal forest- no house, water, bathroom, absolutely nothing but trees.

They immediately began cutting trees that would become the logs for their home. During the building, grandfather miscalculated a swing with the axe. He was severely injured, eventually losing one of his arms.

What would you have done about this time?

He took some time to heal, and then got back to the job at hand. Time was a precious commodity. The house had to be completed before the cold weather set in. My friend's grandfather completed the house in time. They spent that winter, and many more in the house built by a man with one arm.

Has life changed much? Would anyone today take on such a task under such difficult circumstances? They would be a rare individual.

During the 19th and into the 20th Century, many new technologies were explored and developed. Inventions such as the light bulb, indoor plumbing and automobiles began to make their way into the lives of every day people.

Each day in our lives, in the 21st century, we see changes. Change has become so commonplace that we don't even give it much thought. Do you remember how exciting it was to own an eight-track player? Pretty basic and clumsy compared to compact discs and DVDs, right? That was only one small change, a mere forty years ago.

When change occurs in one area of life, it automatically forces change in other parts. Many of the inventions developed in recent times, have had the sole purpose of making life easier. We now have much more time to do other things than work. An invention as "basic" as a light bulb has extended our usable time per day by several hours. We have become so accustomed to such benefits that we have lost sight of how far we have evolved technologically. We take for granted, that which was inconceivable only a relatively short time ago.

Without the pressures of basic survival, the mind does not need to focus on staying alive. The human mind has been trained by thousands of years of developing and implementing strategies for survival. However, the conditioning of the mind to create and process information is still an important factor in our life strategy. No longer needing this skill for survival, the mind still actively thirsts for new information. Unfortunately, I feel we have become distracted with entertainment rather than forging evolution. The void in our mind has become filled with whatever drops into it, usually useless information, due to a lack of discipline and training. People in general, do not realize how their ignorance of the workings of their mind limits the quality of their life. In order to really have a full, well-rounded life on this planet we need to have higher interests than what is going on in Hollywood.

The mind does not care what information it receives; all it knows is that information is received, processed and acted upon. That is its purpose. The outcome has no bearing on its function. Remember the computer idiom: GIGO? (garbage in garbage out)

As consciousness evolves in each person, there comes a time when they realize that improving their level of personal efficiency and quality of life is important for their best well being, hence, the need for the investment in their evolution.

We are seeing a huge display of this evolution in our society today. The newly found interests in yoga, meditation, the arts, writing, and communication are exploding all over the world. Course after course is offered to help individuals delve into their depths in order to find their own path and internal peace.

Human nature, by its own design, is always looking for ways to improve its own lot. We have spent countless centuries floundering without self-awareness, until we finally reached the condition we are in today.

As we learn to look at our lives, we begin questioning the choices we make. We have explored all the lands of our planet and beyond.

Now we can begin to explore the true final frontier, "ourselves."

Fortunately, new tools are becoming readily available that can aid us in taking control of our destinies and improving our lot in life. We are now able to take charge in shaping our lives at a level, never before achievable or comprehendible.

Because we have so much more time, comfort, safety and resources, our minds are now demanding a personal evolution from the inside. We no longer have to contend with the distraction of survival. Our mind needs to fill the void. We can continue to avoid this demand, if we choose, and allow indiscriminant information to continue falling in, but the voice will only grow louder. For our own peace of mind, we must embrace this trail of self-discovery, one patient step at a time. Taking control of the mind is essential.

We are being driven to find the true peace that is ours. Not by avoidance, as was once the method, but by sincere self-exploration, we can attain the inner peace of knowing. True inner peace may be found by getting past the noise of the mind, not by avoiding or suppressing it.

I ask you, why would anyone want to put so much effort into avoiding, when change is inevitable anyway? It is part of the cycle of life we are currently exposed to. So:

Beat the rush!
Be Lazy!
Do it now!
Your evolution is calling!

How do I start my healing process?

Whether or not you are an experienced guru of personal development, the first step I recommend is developing your support group. There are two people I highly recommend for you to commission right from the start. Remember safety first!

They are: A mentor   A counsellor

A mentor is a person who you know well and has a vested interest in your well-being, possibly a close friend. The role of the mentor is to act as a sounding board, a listener.

The mentor does not try to help you in any way, except to be there when you need someone to listen. They do not assist you in trying to solve the dilemma. They only listen or give you a hug if you need one, but no more.

Pick your mentor carefully. The process of personal introspection is a delicate one that can leave you feeling exposed and vulnerable. This person should be one who you trust implicitly. They must appreciate the necessity for a high degree of confidentiality. Generally, this position is not entrusted to anyone whom you have a close relationship with, such as a spouse or a parent. It is too hard for them to be unbiased or remain quiet, as you move through what author Caroline Myss calls the "Dark Night of the Soul."

When determining whom you would choose as a mentor, ask yourself these questions. Try to be as objective as you can.

- Who in my life do I find it easy to speak with that listens to me, but is not judgmental?

- Who is easily available to me? (Lives nearby, has time to help)

- Is this person able to be with me without becoming involved in my struggle?

- Can this person keep their struggle out of mine?
- Can this person be trusted to keep my information private?
- Is this person healthy enough emotionally to be able to be strong while I am feeling afraid?

Could I accidentally choose the wrong person for me?

Yes, and it can have potentially disastrous, or at least limiting results. Be selfish, this work is only for your purpose. You do not have to consider other people's emotional needs at this time and they need to be emotionally stable enough to be there for you without it infringing on their emotional stability.

How do I do this?

Try to find at least two people who could potentially fill the bill. Interview them to see how they fit for you. (What you are asking must also fit for them, as well.) Ask them if they are willing to commit to being your mentor for a given minimum period of time (try three months for a trial period). They must understand and accept the commitment before you start!

A mentor is your own personal anchor while you are weathering the storms in your life.

And how about a counsellor?

A counsellor is a person professionally trained to assist you in the process of understanding your life situation. Depending on the school of thought they are trained in, they can provide important guidance in dealing with many of the issues you are facing.

Choosing a counsellor is just as important. It is not as easy to interview or even meet counsellors prior to having a session with them. Ask friends who are doing personal work if they can recommend anyone they may have worked with. If you have a benefits program associated with your job, check any affiliated resource organizations.

Alternative therapy counsellors, such as myself, can be found via metaphysical information centres (newspapers, book stores, public events, the internet, associations, and churches).

What should I look for in a counsellor?

I feel that the key to a good counsellor is finding a person who you have a good, trusting feeling about. They should act as a guide for you, asking the right questions in order to identify, understand and change the part of your personal expression you are focused on. They should have empathy for your situation, but must stay detached. Counsellors cannot allow their own "smoky glass" to have an impression on your understanding of your issues.

A good counsellor is a guide that assists you in your own work who never takes on the role of cheerleader.

They must be supportive but keep you in the position of the one who is doing the work. They are working as your healing facilitator, but it is you who is the healer. You are in charge of how you change your life, as you are the person who ultimately reaps the benefits.

Are there different kinds of counsellors?

Determining the type of counsellor you want to work with can be tricky. If you are focusing on one particular aspect, you may be able to find one that is a specialist. The inherent danger in selecting this type of counsellor is that they will keep you focused only on that one issue.

By looking at your healing from a more holistic viewpoint, you might be better working with a counsellor who can help you assess your life generally. There may be some piece of information that has no noticeable relationship to the specific area you are trying to change, but has a major impact on it, that could be missed.

A good example of this might be if you were wishing to deal with an issue related to your sexuality. You could go to a sex therapist who would be able to help you to understand your issue and help you cope or make adjustments to overcome the current problem. However, sexual issues usually have to do with power and control that you learned to respond to as a child. The sex therapist could help you heal the symptoms, but would they be able to deal with helping you become aware of the causes?

**If you do not deal with the cause,
you have not really dealt with the problem.**

There are many schools of counselling and as many counsellors. In the macrocosm of the world, they each play an important role. It is up to you to choose what type of counselling suits your needs. Determining the philosophy of the school they trained with is key to understanding if they can help you. Counsellors may include psychiatrists, psychologists, and many schools of professional counselling, clergy, energy healing practitioners and lay counsellors (schooled by life experience).

The results of the treatment styles while working with a counsellor who can help you succeed in getting your life together are more important for you than their education profile, or how much they charge.) Work with someone whom you feel will help you achieve your goals. Both the personality of the counsellor and their treatment style are key components to the success of your healing process. Be sure of whom you place your trust.

How do I choose a mentor and a counsellor? Do I need both?

If you want to have the greatest amount of safety for yourself during your personal work, you will need both. The counsellor will be your primary guide for your introspection. However, they are not always available when you need them, so having a support person, like a mentor, is essential.

So what is the next step once I have my mentor and counsellor in place?

The next step is to decide what you want to work on. If you are not experienced at making life changes, it would be best to find something "easy" to work on. If you are not sure where to start, here are some ways to kick-start.

- Start working with your counsellor right away. Tell the person that you intend to do most of the work on your own, and that you will be continuing the work outside of sessions. Have the counsellor help you select an issue, which you can work with comfortably.

- Take some personal growth courses. This may be a vehicle for developing a relationship with a counsellor as well. Make sure before you sign up for the course, that you know enough about the background of the course facilitator and if this person is associated with any organization. Eliminate any surprises.

- Journaling. Take a big piece of paper and a pen and just begin writing. Do not have any particular focus in mind, as you write. Watch for a theme to develop. It will take the centre of attention in the discourse. Once you have an insight, try to clarify the issue. You may have to work through some degrees of camouflage to find out what is really bothering you. Listen to yourself as you journal. Your thoughts carry clues. Persistence pays!

Okay, I am ready to begin. What now?

Now you are ready to begin the healing process. Remember, it has taken you all of your life to become who you are today. You will need plenty of time to implement any changes. Be kind to yourself. Be honest with yourself. Change is a gradual process. If you expect to complete the changes instantly, you will have very limited long-term success.

Before you begin any sort of inner work, create a safe and comfortable environment. Deal with any distractions such as other commitments, phones, television and other people. If you would like a drink or food, get it. Your comfort is most important in setting the stage in getting through to yourself.

Be honest with yourself about any distractions. Be sure you are not looking for a reason to avoid beginning this work. If you are not ready to change, then wait until you are ready. Your mind may try to make excuses for you to not begin your own personal journey of introspection, as it is feeling threatened by the impending pressure to change the status quo. (These fears may be a good starting point) Be sure you know your motivation, so you can proceed with sincerity.

Presuming you are committed to improving your life now, this is how to get going. It would be helpful for you to set a date to meet with yourself regularly, both for some quiet time, but also for doing your inner work. You will need to give yourself as much support as possible. Setting a regular time for your work will encourage you to keep at it. It is too easy to procrastinate when you do not schedule it in your weekly routine.

Select a time during a specific day or evening and dedicate that time every week to your own personal growth. Let nothing interfere with this commitment. Having this time in your mind, you will automatically prepare yourself for the work you will do.

Your mind will start hunting for projects to fill in that time. Make note of ideas during the week but leave the specific work to that time. If you start trying to solve your life mysteries in a helter-skelter method, your success will be limited and the process convoluted. Focusing yourself on one time slot will keep you organized and in control. Once your time for work arrives, you will be "conditioned" and ready to proceed.

The first step is to get comfortable. Relax and let go of any activity in your head. If you can't relax and clear your head, use journaling to do the clearing. Getting thoughts out of your head and on to paper often dissipates their intensity. When your head stays full of thought, it is a way that your mind tells you that it desires attention to some issue. Give in. It may be where your healing needs to start. This is the beginning of learning how to tell the difference between processing and avoiding.

Make quiet time a regular part of your life. The more you take time to be quiet and listen to your thoughts, the more comfortable you will become with yourself. As your mind recognizes your paying attention to it, the intensity of the thinking will reduce.

Pay attention to your body. Take the time to relax every part starting with your head, neck and shoulders, working downward, eventually releasing your whole body.

Be aware of your ego trying to stop you. It will feel threatened and thus set up roadblocks to keep you at your current level of living.

Let's talk about journaling, since that would be a normal step right now. Most people cannot just sit down and clear their heads right off the bat. If you are facing this situation, get a pen and paper and prepare to write.

To begin, put the pen to the paper and just begin writing. Commit to yourself to keep going for a minimum of ten minutes. Do not concern yourself about what you are writing, just write, even if it is gibberish. You are training your mind to open up and express. Once your mind realizes that you are listening, your writing will settle down and begin to make sense. As you do more and more writing in this manner, it will become easier to vent on paper. Eventually ten minutes may not be enough.

What if I get stuck, you know, writer's block?

If you are feeling stuck, try writing down whatever comes into your head, even if it is "I do not want to do journaling, I hate journaling, I don't know what to write, etc." As you commit your thoughts to paper, your mind will relax and begin to participate.

A very necessary part of the journaling process needs to be carried out prior to putting the pen to the paper. Promise yourself that at the end of the session, you will burn the journaling or at least rip up the paper and dispose of it. Committing to this act allows your mind to feel safe in exploring your deep, dark secrets. It knows that if you regularly destroy the paper, it will be more relaxed and willing to share. Keeping the notes can only act as a reminder of your supposed imperfection. You have had enough reminders for one lifetime. You don't need any more.

Once you are able to get your mind clear of distractions, you can do processes by choice. While you are sitting quietly, choose your focus, and go for it.

Can I use journaling to work on a specific situation?

Absolutely! Write down a history of the event including what happened, where and who was involved. If it is a recent situation, try to recall a similar situation that has occurred sometime in the past. Keep trying to go further back in time, identifying more situations with this common theme.

Try to stay relaxed, listen to your inner guidance. Keep in mind that it may not be the physical situation that is the similarity, but some aspect that is a trigger. The trigger will be something that automatically stimulates one or more of your senses. Amongst thousands of possible triggers, these could include a particular movement such as an abrupt movement of the hand, a smell of perfume or smoke, a red hat, or even a word.

Allow yourself to be aware of all information your senses provide to you. Do not write off any feelings, thoughts, etc just because they don't seem to make sense.

One trigger that I became very aware of, for myself, was whenever anyone waved his or her arm quickly in the direction of my face. I realized that this movement excited a fear response. It reminded me of times where I had been physically threatened as a child. To reprogram myself, anytime I felt this way, I made a purposeful decision to diffuse the reaction by taking a deep breath and relaxing myself as quickly as possible after it had occurred. I told myself to look at the situation that had just occurred and determine whether the person was really trying to threaten me or if I was just reacting to an old stimulus. Eventually, the fear subsided and I was okay with fast hand movements. As I processed this fear, I also used journaling to review my life and access any earlier thoughts and beliefs that related to this trigger device.

In order to move through these kinds of situations, pay attention to how you feel. Do not try to control the situation. Let yourself feel, hear, see, etc. so that you can understand what is going on. Ask yourself questions like: What emotions are you feeling? What thoughts are in your head? Who else is in the story? What is the common thread to the memories? How do you feel in relation to other people in the story? What are they telling you? What is your mind telling you? Every bit of information you can note will help you get to the bottom of the reaction. Concentrating on understanding the reaction brings it to the front of your mind. This allows you to deal with it in the present and reprogram the response.

Keep writing. If you feel the need to cry, scream or get angry, allow yourself do so. When you are in true safety, you can express these feelings, knowing that you will be okay. Write using the feeling as your motivator. Get the feeling and thoughts out of you and onto the paper. Once it is out of your head, it has less control over you. Instead of being a scary giant, let the memory dissolve into a collection of words on a page that will be burned.

Go slowly, and remember, if it is too big of an issue, stop before you lose your sense of safety. See your counsellor, so you can gain more clarity and get a better grip on it.

I feel like I might get stuck in this process even before I get started, so what are some questions that may stimulate some insight?

Try to look at the memory from the viewpoint of who you were at about the age the situation occurred, and then draw it into present time, so you can change its effect in today's world. Looking at the memory as if it was a dream will help you to detach from it.

- What were you trying to do in the memory?
- Did you accomplish it? How?
- What were you really trying to do?
- How did you keep yourself safe in the memory?
- Was there another person involved?
- What do you think they were trying to do?
- Did they understand your intention?
- Did you misinterpret their intention?
- Were you hurt in any way?
- How was the situation resolved, if it was?

If you were in this situation today:
- What triggered that particular memory now?

- How are you feeling?

- What is the level of intensity of the feelings?

- What thoughts are you having?

- How did you react to this same stimulus today?

- How would you handle the situation differently today than before?

- How has this memory affected your life?

- If there was another person in the memory, can you tell what their intention was?

- What response would you prefer to have to similar situations as they occur?

Remember that any situation you are working on is just a memory. Memories are just thoughts. They can not hurt you. Teach yourself to stay detached from them. Listen to and feel what is going on in your mind and body. Pay attention to your thoughts and feelings. They are keys to unlocking the puzzle. Release your attachment to the memories and let them dissipate. The truth will reveal itself.

Know you are safe and that you will get past these feelings.

If you recognize an issue that you just can't get a handle on, work on it with your counsellor. Never try to do something big on your own. Focus on the little stuff until you get used to how the process works. You must decide for yourself whether or not you can handle a situation or not. Be wise.

What do I do once I have completed the session?

Once you are finished, destroy all the notes completely, and then give yourself a nice reward. Congratulate yourself for a job well done. Go do something else that will take your mind off the issue just completed.

Got an example?

Sure always have plenty of those.

John asks, "Why do I feel afraid when I hear doors being slammed?" John sits down, relaxes and focuses on the sound of a door slamming. Quickly he sees a picture of his father barging into the house. His father is very angry. Dad slams the door shut. Mom runs to see what your dad is upset about. Dad starts yelling at Mom. He is drunk again. He starts hitting Mom.

In the picture, John is sitting in the living room watching television, but as the interactions between his parents become louder, his attention is drawn to them. John feels very afraid. Last time this happened Dad hurt Mom. In anger Dad, leaves slamming the door again. Everyone in the house is crying.

While John is reviewing this memory, he stays conscious of how he is currently feeling. He lets himself sense all that is happening but he keeps himself detached so he can observe and learn. He asks himself questions in an attempt to understand what is happening and why he feels scared. John knows he is not his memories.

Once John understands the scene, John moves his mind to the situation that provoked the reaction in the present. He relaxes and lets himself feel. He asks himself more questions. He tries to draw conclusions about the unconscious reaction. As his understanding improves, he comes to the realization that there was no inherent danger in the present situation and that it was only an unconscious reaction.

John takes a deep breath and focuses his mind on his body. He sits still until he relaxes, all the time telling himself that he is safe. He visualizes himself not reacting to door slamming any more. When he feels relaxed and safe, he concludes the exercise.

Once he has finished the visualization, he journals about it to clear his mind. Upon completion, he destroys the papers and heads outside to play with his kids.

Can I expect to resolve and change the issue in one sitting?

To expect radical change is putting too much pressure onto yourself and will likely set you up to fail. Besides, it takes time to integrate the new information into your unconscious mind.

It may take several sessions to really come to grips with any situation. Be okay with it! Going slow is key to success. Make sure you understand what your role is in any issue. You can only change your reaction and thinking. And remember, trying to hold someone else responsible only keeps the issue alive inside you.

Have you got any fun visualization techniques that could be helpful?

Sure, how about this one. Close your eyes and relax. Visualize yourself as you were around the age of 5 years. Beside you, in the picture, view your parents as you saw them at that time. Look at the difference in height between you and your parents. How did you feel? Are they bigger than you?

It is very important to stay out of the intellect. In this exercise please see both your parents as being the same height.

Next, view yourself today. Again, bring in your parents to the picture. Again, compare heights. Be honest with yourself. How tall do you see yourself in comparison to them?

The purpose of this visualization is to assist you in recognizing how you view yourself in relation to others. Since your parents were the dominant authority figures in your childhood, you would see yourself as smaller than them at that time.

If you see yourself smaller or taller than your parents, today, then you are holding yourself in abeyance to others. Continue with the visualization. Bring yourself to the same height as your parents. This action is a symbolic way of telling your mind that you are free to stand in your own power and be your full self.

Every person is entitled to stand in their own authority.

When you finish the picture, you must be at the same height as your parents. Being smaller or taller is not an acceptable outcome. To be truly healthy, you must bring yourself to know that all people are equal in power and authority.

Why is this exercise so important? I have been on my own for a long time.

There is a reason for doing this particular visualization. We all have a masculine and feminine aspect to our personalities. Your parents represent these parts of you. The female represents passive energy and nurturing, while the male side represents action. Your female side is your soft, creative, nurturing side while the male side is the hunter and gatherer, the action taker.

By expressing both sides proportionately, you balance your own nature although you will more naturally express the aspect of the gender of your physical body. (This statement has nothing to do with sexual preferences. It is only to do with expression of personality characteristics)

Achieving this balance takes away much of the unspoken pressure that expresses as anxiety and worry. Isn't much of the confusion we feel about expressing feelings caused by our not knowing what we want or how to get it? In order to be truly fulfilled, the proportionate expression of both sides of our personality is absolutely necessary.

One more point on this subject that is important as well... While expressing the male and female aspects proportionately is important, it is also important to express them appropriately for the situation that is occurring at the time. When you are guiding your children to understand something, a lot of nurturing will go much further than trying to "strong arm" them into achievement with male energy. The same is true if you are trying to teach them how to play baseball. It is far more functional to show them and help them learn the actions that are baseball than to attempt to "coo" them into playing the sport well.

Here's another one that will also help you. I call this the Heart Centre Visualization.

Sit quietly. Let yourself totally relax- body and mind. Visualize a large ball of white light at the centre of your breastbone at its bottom, just above the heart. Feel the energy of the ball. Let the ball grow larger and larger until you are completely encased in it. As it grows, feel it as your own energy system. Keep expanding it until it reaches about two to three feet beyond your body in all directions. Maintain this visualization for several minutes. Open your eyes and take a deep breath. Feel how you have increased your vitality. It is likely that you feel very rejuvenated.

One of the most important goals in your healing is for you to maintain a high level of personal energy. By using this visualization regularly, you will feel more positive and able to deal with life situations. Because it increases your vitality, you will live healthier and be more confident. As you settle in at the higher vibratory rate, you will attract relationships with others who are more positive and healthy. You will take on a much more successful glow.

This visualization is also used to increase your level of personal safety. By increasing your levels of positive energy, you attract more positive events and actually repel negative events. This visualization causes your mind to repel negativity, and attract more optimism.

My granddaughter does something really quite neat, which would be helpful for all of us that increases her positive outlook.

Mya has just turned two years old. She loves playing any kind of game. When she does something really well, she jumps about with her arms up in the air while yelling "Yay." She gets so excited, every time she does something really well. Because she gets so excited, she learns very rapidly and is developing healthy self-esteem.

That is such a great lesson for all of us. Honouring our achievements by celebrating them is such a powerful tool for improving our self-esteem. Giving ourselves permission to revel in our achievements is so healthy for us. It is such a simple tool for feeling good. We all like to be recognized when we do well. Who should celebrate your success the most, but you? When we celebrate our successes, we attract more success. When we are successful, we feel better. Stressful situations lose their power. So "Yay!" Right Mya?

The flip side of this coin is in not undermining ourselves when we do something in a less than satisfactory manner. There is an old saying that tells us, that we only really learn by making mistakes. Life is a process of making mistakes. We keep making one after another until we find the right outcome, then we go on to a new mistake. (But this is okay, right?)

When a potential mistake is looming on the horizon, remember, we are not obligated to act it out because:

We are not our thoughts, egos, emotions or mind
They are separate from us.

Therefore we are not the mistake either. If the mistake can be caught before it actually happens, then it won't occur. The mistake is only caused by faulty thinking. In order to prevent it, one needs to be able to detach from the event, so that it can be viewed without becoming the event.

When mistakes are viewed as learning experiences, there is no need for punishment. It is only when a mistake is made on purpose that it will result in a repercussion. The law of cause and effect is always true. However, we can mitigate the outcome by depersonalizing the action, so that we can make a conscious choice. We might not choose correctly, but an incorrect conscious mistake is still better than repeating an unconscious habit.

When you make a mistake, try to stand back and look at it objectively. Do not allow yourself to go into any old habits of putting yourself down. Human beings make mistakes, all of us, no exceptions. Recognize what choice you made. If you can discover why, so much the better, as there was likely an unconscious motivator, such as a core belief in play. C'est la vie. (Such is life.) After you assess the situation, give yourself a big hug and go "Yay!" Then try again.

You always have choice

Do you have any suggestions concerning things I should not do during my healing process?

There are a number of issues that are of importance. The most important concern that I will raise is this,

Do not give up on yourself.

You are doing this work for your benefit. Everyone else will benefit from your choices, but do it for yourself.

I feel that you should keep confidentiality about the work you are doing. Only tell those who need to know. I feel that your spouse is the one person you should inform. Keeping this personal work secret from him or her is, in my mind, tantamount to not being in the relationship. They should be part of your support group, for they have the most to gain, outside of yourself. Any person, who is not close to you or possibly will not support you in your quest, should not be included in your circle. You need to garner all the support you can. Do not take the chance of having your confidence undermined.

When you are speaking with anyone about the inner work you are doing, keep the discussion generic. Do not be specific about what issue you are working on, at least until you feel you have a handle on it. By speaking specifically about the issue, you reduce the energy of the process and leave yourself vulnerable to other people's opinions on the matter (except your mentor and counsellor).

What about negative thinking? I am really good at that!

As we all are. We seem to learn really well how to put ourselves down. Do not allow negative thinking to take over your life. As you come to more self-awareness, you will observe many aspects about yourself that you may not be happy with. They are just "stuff." They are not you.

Honour the negative thoughts by realizing that they are a protective safety tactic. Some part of you fears making changes, so it tries to make the work you are doing look bad, so you will quit. Try to find out what the fear is about, and then deal with the issue. Assure yourself that you are safe and capable of enduring whatever you need to, in order to make any necessary changes.

If your mind is whirling with negative thoughts, step back, take a deep breath, and do the heart centre visualization. If the thought persists, do some journaling on it.

**Remember, this is an adventure;
your life is not at stake if you do not change.**

I will share with you now a powerful technique that is strongly impacted by a firm understanding of the concept that we are not our thoughts. By separating ourselves dynamically from our thoughts, we can change how they affect us.

It is my belief that we do not actually rid ourselves of any beliefs, but we can change the outward expression they have provoked. By consciously changing the outcome, the result can be beneficial rather than challenging and limiting. By taking the power away from the emotional patterns of our thoughts, they can return to their inherent truth and be used as a positive influence.

A Story About Bob

Bob was a very timid person. He shook visibly anytime he was required to speak in a formal setting. He avoided social situations, almost to the point of being a hermit. Deep inside Bob, a voice called to him. It was a desire to escape from this prison. He looked at other people, and longed for the sharing he saw. He dreamed of having a mate by his side forever, whom he could travel through life with. With her, he could take on the world and provide the very best for his family.

But, alas, Bob was a "nobody." He lived alone in a tiny suite in a house. When not at work, he spent all of his time alone. Even in his job, he hid himself off in a corner. His mind kept telling him, that nobody wanted to be near him and that he had nothing to offer.

His mind kept him segregated. Nobody could come near. Then one day, a new girl came to work in his office. Sally was beautiful, soft spoken and friendly. Bob realized she was the one he wanted. Of course, he never said anything to Sally. He remained, as always, a wallflower.

Sally fit easily into her new work environment. She made friends with everyone, except Bob. Every time she tried to speak with him, he froze and turned away.

Finally, one day, Bob knew he had hid long enough. He could bear his isolation no longer. He walked up to Sally's desk, and began slowly speaking with her. Sally smiled a radiant smile that immediately lit up Bob's heart.

Mustering all the strength he possessed, Bob forced

himself to ask Sally out on a date. A thousand pounds of pressure were released when she said yes. Bob's mind soared with happiness.

From that moment, Bob made up his mind that he would do whatever it would take to not crawl back inside himself. He began looking inside himself for strength.

Bob began to work with a counsellor and a new understanding of who he was began to appear. Bob was not an unlovable person who needed to hide in the corner of life. He realized that he just didn't understand how to interact with others.

Eventually, he joined a public speaking group. Even though terror raged in his mind, he forced himself to get up and speak. It took him a long time to find any degree of comfort in his new hobby, but he kept trying. He developed many friends in the group. The support was just what he needed to finally lay his walls (protective barriers) to rest. Although he never wanted to be a great speaker, he certainly became more confident as his ease with speaking increased.

As he became more comfortable with his "new self" and Sally became a more prominent participant in his life, he looked closely at his persona. He knew that overreacting to his new lifestyle could be catastrophic, so, through much focus and introspection, he realized that it would suit him best to allow himself to be the soft-spoken, passive person he had always expressed. The difference now was that Bob could relax and let other people into his life. The wallflower was gone.

Sally suggested that Bob should consider becoming a counsellor. With his "easy to be with" personality and his compassionate nature, she felt others would be comfortable disclosing their concerns to him. She told him that she was amazed how easily he could understand the complexities of being human, and that he had helped her understand her life to a much deeper degree.

A light began to shine in Bob's mind. He knew she was right. As he recounted the frustrations of his old life style, he knew that with his experience and new understanding, he really could help others. He could hardly believe how he was so similar to his old self and yet a totally different person. The perceived weakness of only a few years before was now the basis of his new career and his new strength.

Is there a "real me" under all this heavy stuff? Could I become someone I am not?

It is important as you make changes in your life to be really aware of the basis of your personality. BE REAL. If you move yourself too far away from your native self-expression, you may feel that you have created yourself into another person. This is not the goal. Be assured that you innately know who you are.

The goal is to reveal and embrace who you are and clear the path for your own true expression.

Although we may at times feel that we should just dump this persona for a new one, I feel that it is very important that we realize and accept that there is nothing really wrong with being who we see ourselves as. It is only the expression that needs a tune up.

Everybody has aspects of themselves that they "do not like."

It is okay to not like the expression; however, it is vital that we accept loving ourselves. Nobody is perfect. If we were perfect, there would be no reason to grow. Be fair and kind to yourself and give yourself the room and support you need.

As you evolve, people will notice. This will stimulate them. Your evolution will create a domino effect for others. Without actually telling anyone what you have been doing, you will cause others to treat you differently.

When others feel you acting differently and treating them differently, they will automatically change as well. Just smile and know that it all has been worthwhile.

Isn't life great? Once we have the tools that we need to help us clear out the illusions we have lived with for so many years, we will spontaneously begin to see life from a more healthy perspective. Since our parents have played such an important role in our development, our view of them is key to developing a healthier life.

Honouring Mom and Dad

A cautionary note: This is an important exercise that will help you to discover and re-work the foundations of your feelings about your life. Once you start writing a letter to your folks, you will definitely find all kinds of issues to work on. I suggest that you keep writing letters to them until you can honestly write one that demonstrates that you now "own your stuff."

Every person has a symbolic "Mom and dad" or "male and female side" to their personality. The more easily we can see each of these sides and be comfortable with them, the more peace and progress we will have in our life. Owning your own inner mom and dad is such a great and powerful experience for your own self healing, so please take advantage of this learning opportunity.

This exercise does not require actual interaction with your "parents" and you are definitely not to send these letters to them. This exercise is only for your benefit. It is designed to help you access the mom and dad inside of you, in your own makeup. If you have issues with either or both of your parents, it is essential that you resolve them, if for nothing else than finding your own peace of mind.

If you either do not have access to your parents due to death, geographical distances or because you are not feeling prepared to interact with them directly, you may still work through this exercise. Your counsellor will be very happy to work this one through with you.

Loving yourself and doing what is best for you is always the motivation.

Just so you really understand the exercise I have inserted a letter I wrote to my mom and dad. Let's see how you do. You can do as many as you want until you get the clarity you desire.

Dear Mom and Dad,

It seems so long ago since we last spoke. So much has happened since you passed on. Life is good for me. Well, actually, I have these issues that bother me a lot. But, I have finally decided to deal with them.

I felt very angry when you died. You left me here alone. I didn't know what to do. When I felt the anger, I thought it was you I was mad at. You didn't tell me life was going to be this hard. You didn't teach me how to get by very well.

Once the anger subsided, I decided to seek counselling. Life just didn't feel very good. My counsellor helped me to see that the anger I was feeling was misdirected. He also told me that you didn't plan to make my life come out this way. I am the way I am because; I subconsciously chose to see things this way. As you always told me, I definitely have my own mind.

When I realized that there was no fault to blame you for, a very heavy pressure lifted from my mind. You were trying to get through life in the best way you knew how. Why didn't you know more about raising kids? Why wasn't anyone able to tell you about life? Did you even know to ask?

I tried blaming God, too, but that didn't work either. My counsellor said that blaming God was the same as blaming you. He said we come to this life to learn, to experience and to work things out. If we came here and didn't have the challenges we face, there would be no purpose for us being born. Boy, I guess I must like to learn. This life has sure been a challenging one, so far.

I learned that by honouring you, I am also honoring myself. You were role models for me in my school of life, and your parents were the same. I know now that by accepting you for the people you were, I can release my anger. The anger was a tool I used to hide from my own feelings of fear and inadequacy. I couldn't see what a good person I was and how much I actually knew about surviving. Fear was just a shadow I was hiding behind.

I used to think I was safe if I felt angry. I could keep the whole world out, just by thinking about how rotten my life was. I wanted to know why you did this to me. I wanted to know why you couldn't make my life as perfect and wonderful, as other people had. Why did it seem that I was the only one who had to suffer? I never saw any body else suffer the way I did.

I didn't stop to realize that other kids had to live in families where they were physically and emotionally abused or one parent was an alcoholic. Lots of kids didn't even have enough food to fill their bellies at suppertime.

I am glad now, when I think of how well you provided for me. Maybe you weren't perfect but my emotional bruises are small and my belly was kept full.

Now that I have learned how to feel truly safe, I can see what a trickster my mind was. I still get stuck there sometimes, but at least now, I can recognize when my mind wants to take me to the "game." I get to choose whether I want to play or not. Life seems so much easier without the anger. I was just scared. I know that now. I didn't know what to do. It all seemed so real.

Mom and Dad, you didn't know any more about life than I do now, but I expected you to know everything. You lived by what you had learned. WHY has it taken so long for people to figure out that we have to work at building a life? WHY has nobody told us that we can change how we think and therefore change our lives? WHY weren't there any Better Parenting courses?

I know you did all you could. Your heart was in the right place. It was wrong of me to blame you for my weaknesses. You were just trying to get through life, as best you could with much fewer tools than we have today.

I try now to remember how you were always there for me when I got hurt. Your hugs always made me feel better. It was amazing how a little kiss on the forehead magically healed my wounds. It almost made it worthwhile getting hurt. Thanks Mom.

I remember talking with Grandma. She told me many times how you were feeling frustrated because you couldn't do better. She said to you, "Never mind trying to figure life out, just do what you have to do to keep us in line and fed. Everything else will work out. Life is about surviving, so never mind worrying about stuff we can do nothing about." It must have been tough feeling that you could do better, even though there was no support from anyone. Where could you have turned? I love you, Mom.

Did you and Dad love each other, or even like each other, for that matter? People didn't walk out on their "responsibilities" very often in your day, did they? Not like today. Were you and Dad friends, or did you ever even have enough time or energy to find out?

Hey Dad! And I am saying my life is tough! What was going on when we were growing up? Were jobs easy to get? Did your job pay enough to get by on? Were there any wars or other heavy political actions happening that took you away from us? It must have been very hard living without Medicare and Social Services, knowing that if you couldn't provide for us adequately, there was no social net. I sure don't remember suffering.

It must have been tough for you, having us dependent on you for our survival. It must have been hard knowing that you couldn't, just once, take the day off and go for a walk in the forest. You taught me strong work ethics as I watched you go off to work every day. I'll bet it was frustrating having to "fight dragons" all day while you thought Mom was at home watching soap operas or having lunch with the girls. It's too bad you couldn't trade with Mom for a few days so you could each see how challenging each of your lives were, and how dependent you were on each other to do your part.

Is it true that you had to work long hours every day, often six days a week, just to keep us fed? That sure must have left little time for spending time with us. It's no wonder you guys seemed to be grouchy all the time. It must have been hard working so hard, having no time to play or relax. That television must have been a great soother for you after a long day.

I guess even when you did have a day off; there must have been a whole lot of work to do around the house. There sure weren't the modern conveniences back then that we have today, was there? And we had the nerve to complain! I realize now how much you did for me that I never thanked you for. Thanks Dad.

I know that if you had a magic wand, there would be lots of things you would change about our lives. Now I see that you had issues that distorted your way of thinking and living. And you didn't know anything like we know today about fixing them. You learned how to react to situations by watching your parents and others. You learned to control us by yelling at and hitting us, because that was the way it was always done. You were yelled at and hit too, so your mind reproduced this action as if it was natural, just like loving us. I know you told me many times, you felt so useless as a parent. But you would be proud of me now, if you could see me today, and I owe much of my life today to you and Mom.

Now that I am starting to understand my responsibility to myself and to others, my sense of what I value in life is changing. Life would not be such a great adventure if I didn't have my friends and family to share life with. Now that I am learning to be easier on myself, I seem to find that everyone around me is happier too. I never realized before how much my attitudes affected others.

The more I realize how protected children are today compared to when we were little, it is easier to see how much we need to quit complaining about how hard done by we are and just get on with healing ourselves, so we can realize our capacity.

Now that I am a parent, I am especially thankful for all the things that you took the time to teach me when I was little. I may have resented some of the things that happened back then but I can now look back fondly at the many experiences that I take for granted today, that you had to work so hard to get me to understand. I know you were doing your best to protect me and teach me how to look after myself.

Isn't it amazing how hard it is to teach a kid to tie up his shoe laces? I remember standing at the doorway, getting ready to leave for my first day of school. We both looked at each other completely baffled. You couldn't comprehend why I was not doing up my shoes, and me looking incredulously at these ropes sticking out of my shoes! I thought for sure I would trip on them when I tried to walk. Suddenly you realized I had never tied up laced shoes before. I didn't know how to tie my laces!

Dad, Did I get in the way when you were working in your shop? I remember asking you a million questions, trying to understand what you were doing. It sounded so comforting to hear you using saws, drills and hammers. I still love to do woodworking. It reminds me so much of the times I watched you creating your masterpieces. Remember that beautiful bookcase you made that I tried to copy? Mine looked like a pile of scrap compared to yours. But it stood proudly in your bedroom corner for years.

As I got older, you provided me with a basis for much of how I define my adult life. My love of nature, photography, camping, philosophy, even the foods I prefer.

I am glad I am coming to be my own person more and more though, Dad. Like all people, you reacted differently to many situations in your life than I now prefer to respond to, in kind. I consciously choose to make alternative choices. I am sure my children will do the same. I hope you understand that I need to know who I am. I cannot just be a reflection of you and Mom. My life is different from yours, so I have to make my own choices. I hope you can trust me when I say that I know what I am trying to do. Having your support would make the load a whole lot lighter.

Mom and Dad, it has taken many attempts to actually write this letter to you, where I completely stayed in my heart. Every other time, I found my mind wandering back to the old hurts. Gradually, though, I was able to overcome the habit of blaming you for my failings, and those thoughts fell away. It was only then that I could let myself love you without the partitions I have hidden behind in the past. I thank both of you for giving birth to me and for providing me with the tools I now have. I thank you for supporting me now, even though you are gone, helping me find the strength to be who I truly am. Without your teachings, I would have nothing to base my life lessons on.

I honour you, Mom and Dad.

Love,

Your son

This sounds like a really powerful tool. Is this something we can share with others or is it best to keep it to ourselves?

I suggest that you do not send these letters to your parents or anyone else except perhaps your counsellor, at least until you get to the final copy. Remember, this is your learning process, not anybody else's. It is you that has chosen to change your life. Others may not even realize changes were necessary or possible. Unless your parents are particularly enlightened, they may not understand your intention or have a desire to talk about the past in a meaningful way for you. Even the most positive and loving letter may be beyond their scope of understanding and trigger their own fears. Just tell them you love them and leave it at that.

Why does making peace with our parents seem to be such a big thing nowadays?

It seems to be a peculiarity of the Baby Boomer and newer generations that, as we get older, knowing ourselves is becoming more important. Part of this seems to require making peace with our parents. Once they have passed on, we are out of time. Of all the wishes that I hear from people whose parents are no longer with us, having the chance to make peace with their parents is their greatest longing. Unfortunately time does not wait … and neither should this healing opportunity.

Do you recommend that everyone do this, even if they had a really challenging relationship with their parents?

No matter what your childhood was like, your parents still deserve to be loved and recognized as "human beings in training."

Remember it is crucial to:

Know the difference between the person and the action.

You do not have to love or like what "they did," but in your heart you will always love Mom and Dad, no matter what. There is not one parent in the whole world that would have honestly wished anything bad for their child. Sometimes habits and unconscious reactions just get in the way. Fortunately,

We now have the tools to re-find our truth, so that we do not have to continue old family patterns.

A young boy in the neighbourhood had developed a habit of taking pretty scarves from wherever he found them. It did not matter if the scarf was lying on the street or in a house he was visiting. He had to have it. He never really thought about whether taking them was right or wrong. He was only a child. The scarves were beautiful. He liked how they felt.

No one really noticed his habit. It went on for a couple of years until one day; he was visiting at the home of a friend down the street. While he was there he had noticed and pocketed a beautiful silky blue bandana. This was to be the last prize for his collection. The scarf belonged to his friend's sister. When she discovered it missing, she let loose and began interrogating and inspecting everyone present.

Of course, when it came to the boy, he tried to deny taking the scarf. The sister grabbed at him, reaching into his pockets. All the fire inside the girl boiled to the top. She started hitting him, all the while screaming at him for being a thief.

The girl's mother came running and broke the two apart. Sending the boy home after telling him that there would be discussions with his parents, the mom sat the girl down. After helping her relax and get control over herself, she began:

"What was it that got you angry?"

"My scarf was missing and I wanted to wear it."

"How did you feel when you discovered it gone?"

"Angry. I don't like when I can't find something."

"How did you feel when you found the scarf in the boy's pocket?"

"I felt extremely hurt and angry. He had no right to take it; I didn't like him because he took it."

"Did you like him before this happened?"

"Yes, he was always fun to have around."

"Is he the same person in both situations?"

"Yes, but I still don't like him for taking my bandana!"

"Can you see that it is not him that you are angry at but what he did? He is still the same child you previously enjoyed?"

"Oh, then I should not be mad at him. I should just let him take my stuff?"

" No my dear, what I am pointing out is that it would be better for all of us if you can separate his action that made you feel angry, from who he is as a person. He is still the same little boy. I want you to understand that if you are going to feel angry, direct it to the true cause, not the person. I will speak with his mother so she can help him. I want you to learn to love people despite their actions.

When you learn to separate the person from the action, it is much easier to see people for who they are, rather than what they do. This makes it much easier to love people, and yourself. All people make bad choices somewhere in their lives. They still deserve to be loved. Through love, they can heal and make changes. Through punishment and blame, they will only continue their habit. He has been a good lesson for you."

The next step of this exercise is to write a responding letter from your dominant parent. Put yourself in their shoes and try to imagine what they would say to you about their life. Here is the one I wrote from my Mom.

Dear Son,

Now that you are older, it is much easier to tell you how I feel. Part of this will be telling you about the family you were born into. It has not been an easy life.

I love you and am very proud of you. I know many times over your life you have probably wondered if I even cared if you lived. I want you to know and understand right now, that there never was a time in my life that I didn't love you from the bottom of my heart. I am so grateful that you were born, and that you are my son.

Life has been very hard. I do not know why it had to be this difficult. Your father and I tried our best to provide for you, but life seems to have a habit of not turning out the way we wanted it to.

Your Dad and I met after only a few years out of high school. We married very soon after that, mostly because our parents wanted us to. In our day, we did what we were told; there was no room for argument or discussion, especially with our parents.

Starting out was very challenging. I had finished secretarial school, so I had already found a job. Your Dad wanted to go to university and actually had completed all the entrance tests, but as soon as we got together, you decided to join us.

Even though your dad saw his chance for getting an education going by the wayside, he was excited at the idea of becoming a father. So, he took a job at the local factory during the day and attended school at night. It took him five gruelling years to finally get his diploma in business.

Life was much easier when he got his promotion to department manager in the mill since the pay was much better. But your dad still was not around much because, instead of night school, he had to work longer hours.

There weren't many places or people to talk with about raising children. It was literally sink or swim. I asked my mom for suggestions, but she made it sound like I wanted to be trained to look after inmates in a prison, not raising my family. I knew there had to be ways to help each of you grow, as individuals, but I couldn't find them.

I found it so frustrating, so frustrating that I often lost my temper. I am sorry you were the one who received most of it. With your dad off working so much, I was left to figure things out on my own. You seem to be doing well, so I guess in the long run I must have done okay. It sure didn't feel like it at the time. Raising kids properly is a big job.

Once you were born, I had to quit my job. Although I resigned myself to be a housewife, I did not like it. I wanted to work for a few years before we had children. We could hardly afford the little one bedroom apartment we had, but with you coming along, we had to move to a bigger place. Grandpa helped out by loaning us money for the down payment on our first home. It took us forever to pay him back, but we did. We had to go without many things for a long time because money was so tight.

Do you remember when you got so upset because Johnny's family got a colour TV and we didn't? You scowled for weeks. I was so angry with you, but I just couldn't explain. How could I make a 7-year old understand that we just didn't have any extra money?

And that time that you and your brothers decided to go on strike until we promised to take you to Disneyland at spring break. You thought you were a united force until I threatened to quit making supper in retaliation. You were the first one to the table that night. It seemed that you kids just could not understand that money doesn't grow on trees.

It wasn't until you were all in your teens that we were finally able to afford a holiday together, but that didn't work out very well. You were so used to sticking around the neighbourhood all summer that when the chance to get away was offered, none of you wanted to go. There just seemed to be no way to win.

Even though Dad did not have to serve in the military, life was bitterly affected by the war. It was far away but every family was affected. First, men disappeared to far away countries with some never coming back. Then people, here at home, didn't want to support the war any more. They became afraid of each other. The solidarity of past generations was replaced by freethinking; only nobody seemed to know how to let other people think freely.

People began to emigrate from other countries. Their life styles conflicted with our established rules. We felt afraid. It took many years before we could comfortably walk down the street again. I am sure our new neighbours must also have felt awkward too.

It must have been hard for you. You just wanted to play with the little boy down the street. What he looked like did not matter to you; he was just another child near your age. We sure let our silly fears get in the way, didn't we?

It was tough staying married to your dad. It took many years for me to come to terms with the events in my life. I was looking forward to having fun with my friends for a few years before getting serious about life. Our parents had a different plan for our lives though. Adding to the frustration, you were born before your dad and I even had time to become friends or to fall in love. Fortunately, I liked your dad. He was a good person, even though he was very hard to live with much of the time. I think of how hard he worked and how much he gave up for us. He deserved to be grouchy.

I didn't make it easy for him either. I recognize now, how I took my frustration out on him. For years, I acted like a spoiled child. I resented having my freedom taken away from me. He was the easiest target, so I took it out on him. We got so used to attacking each other that chiding each other became habitual. We didn't even realize we were hurting each other.

It was years before we finally figured out how to raise each of you kids. You were all so different. If I could go back to the beginning, I would surely do things differently, but, as I came to understand, albeit many years too late, our job was to provide you with the foundation to build your life on. We could not be perfect parents. There was no such thing. We were not even concerned about being perfect, we just wanted to survive. We did our best, considering how things were. It does not matter how hard we look back at our pasts we cannot change anything.

I love you son. I have truly enjoyed sharing my life with you. I truly wish that you could find all the answers to your life and to raising your children while you still have time on your side. You have a lot to give to the world. I am proud of you.

Love

Mom

As the grand finale before completing the letter, include a paragraph that completes this thought:

And I know you loved me because ...

This part of the project helps to cement the positive feelings needed to ensure that this exercise is a beneficial healing opportunity. Sometimes it is hard to really accept the good side of a parent, but no matter how traumatic you believe your childhood was, there still were hints of love.

I didn't include it in my letter because I wanted to save it until now. So I will now add that paragraph.

And I know you loved me because, even when you got mad at me, you hugged me after you finished scolding me. I also knew you loved me when, you got up early in the morning on weekends to take me to hockey. And most of all, you always knew to make spaghetti and meatballs when you knew I needed cheering up. Thanks Mom

Finding the beauty and love in your relationship with your dominant parent is key to finding the power in your own dominant side. Hanging on to positive memories of

your parents helps keep you going during tough times.

The better you can hang on to the positive, loving side of life, the more inner strength you will have for dealing with life's challenges. It is too easy to poison our minds with negative thinking. Using the strength available through this exercise will help keep you clear and powerful ... and making good choices.

The greatest strength you own is achieved through making peace with yourself.

Honouring your mom and dad is absolutely essential if this process is to be complete.

Throughout this journey, we have been assembling tools for one purpose.

Getting to know and express your true self

The Final Frontier – Embracing the Blend

R emember the opening line of Star Trek - "Space, The Final Frontier?"

Gene Roddenberry, Star Trek's creator, changed our lives with that now so famous line. I feel that he inspired much more than an interest in life on a space ship. He and his crew help to engender the mindset that there is more to life than the here and now. Life is infinite. All we have to do is "Get past the Cling-ons!"

In truth, our minds are the "Final Frontier," the last place for us to explore and truly know. Without knowing and taking control of our own mind, there is no conscious reality for us. Without attaining a relatively high degree of awareness and mastering the old beliefs, we can not be truly in control of the most powerful asset we own. We will remain puppets to the old thinking patterns of our pasts. We will never really know the other "final frontiers" if we can not train ourselves to get beyond the limitations we have placed on ourselves for the sake of survival. Our realities, all of them, are a product of our belief systems. Until we gain control of our beliefs we cannot know the truth about anything.

Sound inviting to stay where you have been? For your sake, I hope not!

As I have stated previously, life is changing very rapidly during this current period of mankind. Either you can resist and try to stay the same or you can go with the flow. Either way, life will continue to evolve..... and you are going to change.... just by the mere fact that you are living today. Knowing and embracing your true self is not only the key to survival, it is also the key to all the joy and happiness that is truly yours, just because you are you. So let's admit we are on board the train and go for the ride.

Embrace your life and soar to new heights, just for the excitement of being alive.

"We must go beyond that which mankind has ever known before."

Remember Bob? He visited with us a couple of chapters ago. He definitely had some issues that needed fine-tuning. The beauty is that he did face himself and his issues. Here's the "whole" story about Bob. Have a look in yourself and find the "Bob" in you.

Bob was born into a large family who lived together on a small farm. As the oldest child of seven children, he took the brunt of responsibility for everything that happened in the home.

Bob remembered his father as an alcoholic, a very angry alcoholic. His strongest memories were of his father raging like a bull, screaming angrily and striking out at anything and anyone who got in his way every time life threw up a challenge.

His mother was a woman who Bob loved dearly, a soft, sweet woman who spent her life totally absorbed in the raising of her children. He remembered a quiet, strong woman who stayed focused on her mission, never allowing the mayhem caused by her husband to distract her from raising her children as best as she was able.

When his father was drunk, which seemed to be more and more often as years went by, Bob learned to stay out of the way. Too many times as a young child, he had not been quick enough. He suffered at the hands of his father, either through beatings or by being put to work like a slave.

He tried to turn to his mother for help as the terror increased but she could do little. With six other children to protect, she could only help soothe his pains in the aftermath.

As Bob entered his teens, he felt the power of his oncoming manhood. He tried to stand up to his father, to protect his siblings and his mother. Not understanding the anger in his father's mind, he only set himself up for unbelievably worse misery. His father now saw Bob as competition to his authority. Anytime he could make life miserable for Bob, he did. His father believed that he could break this impudent boy by whipping him regularly for whatever reason he could justify in his mind.

Bob did his best to appease his father, but it did no good. His father had an unspoken, unbendable agenda.

Finally, one day, Bob snapped. He knew in his mind that he could never change the events in his life. The power of this angry man was too much. Bob withdrew into himself. The world was an unsafe place, so his mind took him to the only place where survival was possible... inside himself.

Learning to remain disconnected from the outside world allowed him to function, much like a robot. One shovel full at a time, with not a word spoken, Bob saw his father win over his power. At least the beatings and the horrible shouting matches ended, for him. With seven other people in the home, his father moved on to any other person naive enough to engage with him, revelling in the knowledge that he had been victorious over Bob.

His mother always had a ready smile for Bob. She kept the cookie jar full of wonderful treasures, so that whenever he was feeling sad; a cookie from her loving hand would lift him up and make life bearable. He tried to speak with his mother about his feelings, his anger and frustration toward his father, but she just could not help. Although, she loved her children dearly and would have given her life for any one of them, she knew no other method than to submit to this man who terrorized her family. She too had stood up to him once. She learned much more quickly than Bob. Her strength came from knowing to do what you do best, out of harm's way.

Getting away from this home as soon as possible seemed to be the only way to survive. His very strong character pushed him to do well in school. Even though he did not have a lot of time for homework, Bob excelled in school. He did so well that he was nominated for scholarships to several colleges.

Rather than choosing the college that provided the best courses for him, he chose the school that was farthest from home. He just wanted to get away. He did not care what he had to endure; it could not be any worse.

Never having learned to socialize, school became a long struggle of classes and studying. Bob lived quietly in a basement suite near the campus, his daily regimen broken up only by his part-time job at a local hardware store where he stocked shelves late into the night, when everyone else had gone home.

Sometimes a break in the routine of his life allowed time for a walk in the local park or a weekend camping trip, always by himself. Other people seemed to rarely even notice his existence.

As his college days concluded, his next move was into the corporate head office of the hardware company. Without realizing it, he had accepted a position where he would continue his solitary existence, hidden in the corner of the computer department.

Somewhere deep inside this person burned a flame, a flame that would not go out, no matter how bad life got or how big the walls were around him. For years, dreams about sharing his life with other people surfaced in the night. As he travailed his lonely path, he sadly watched passersby, longingly wishing that someone could find an opening in his "fortress."

Many times over the years, people had tried to enter Bob's inner sanctum, only to find the passageway blocked and the door firmly closed. Fear had done a magnificent job of protecting this person from the terrors of life, but the flame kept burning.

In his youth, books were not a great friend or healer. One has to have time to build a relationship with friends. Books were only tools for acquiring information as he studied in the infrequent moments between his father's unrelenting lists of demands. However, now that he was older and time was his own, the relationship blossomed.

At first his interests led him to science fiction and fantasy but he found them unfulfilling. Travel and history only reminded him of his need to run away from his past.

One day, at a local bookstore, he let himself wander into sections he had never noticed before. He became mesmerized by the writings of the great mystics. Very slowly he began to understand that his life was a journey, an evolution. He realized that if his life was to improve, it was up to him to decide where he wanted to go and what he had to do to get there.

Life did not permit change easily. Like most people, by the time he was into adulthood his life was well entrenched with habits that appeared unrelenting. It felt like there were two opposing forces trying to control his life.

As Bob continued his investigation, he came to realize that the opposing forces really had no control over him, unless he chose to let them. He began to see how he had let them run amok and turn his life into a path of continuous turmoil, inhibiting any chance of happiness. He came to know that his mind used confusion as a protective device. It was easier, his mind thought, to keep life the same, than to take a chance on something new.

Slowly his life began to change. Bob developed an association with a counsellor who understood and related to his needs and his goal of true freedom. Step-by-step, day by day the spiralling evolution spun faster and wove a new web.

Realizing that many of his unconscious habits protected him from old memories, Bob practiced stepping back and learning to feel his true self. From this vantage point, he began to see the difference between himself and the perceptions his mind had created. He began to feel the power that was him. His newfound strength roared throughout his being like a fire in a tinder dry forest. It was becoming a raging inferno.

When Sally came to work for his employer, he knew it was time to come out of hiding, but it took many months for him to finally take the chance. After all, it was easy to just do the work in his head, away from everyone else.

Life has a way of forcing our hand, and Sally was the determining factor. If everything he had read and practiced were to be of any value, his life now demanded he put it into action.

As he watched from his cubicle in the office, Bob revelled in the site of his dream. Her smile turned up the flame in his heart to almost unbearable temperatures. Her laughter drove his mind to near insanity. Finally, he knew that the walls had to come down or he might not survive.

In his mind, Bob practiced what he wanted to say to Sally, hoping he could say the right thing. His mind raced with thoughts of rejection and want. Confusion reigned and muddied up his mind. Through his studies he knew this was just a game his mind played in order to keep him safe. Deep in his mind, though, he knew that Sally was no threat, taking the chance to know her was his salvation. He had to speak to her. He had to make his life change …and for the better. Right now.

Sally was sitting alone in her office, when Bob finally made the move. It was almost time to leave for the day. Bob knew that if she rejected him, at least he could escape and prepare for his life in solitary. A part of him still needed protection and held him back. An escape plan seemed necessary so that he could muster the strength to break the ice.

As he turned into the doorway of her office, Sally turned and smiled at him. Without waiting for him to speak, she reached out her hand to him and invited him to sit. Quietly he accepted the invitation. Still looking at her, he fumbled his way to the nearest chair, moving with legs that felt like lead. Sally began chatting with him casually, magically lassoing his heart. Bob responded as his barriers began to melt like icicles hanging from the branch of a tree during a warm winter wind. He couldn't believe, as he sat there, how easy it was to be with her. Never before had Bob ever felt such comfort and connection with another human being. He liked it.

Time slipped by, as the conversation continued. Finally looking around the office, they both realized that everyone else had gone home. Embarrassed for detaining her for so long, Bob apologized and stood up preparing to leave, but something stopped him. Ever so quietly he returned to looking at Sally and asked her to join him for dinner.

The walls of the fortress became more transparent as Bob's life became entrenched with Sally's. He was determined to live a normal life. Sally supported him in his drive for self-knowledge. He continued working with his counsellor.

Step-by-step, Bob reviewed his life. His greatest strength came when he was able to detach from his memories of childhood, to look at them, as they really were.... the lessons that unveiled who he really was and what he came to this life to complete.

He learned that rather than looking at his father as an angry drunk who beat on him mercilessly at every opportunity, he saw him as a person who was so afraid of not being able to survive in a world that he viewed as overwhelming and very scary.

It was not easy for Bob to come to this view of his father. He had to muster up a lot of courage to get past the automatic veils that curtained his view of "Dad" and look at him as a person for the first time, a soul who taught him to survive in a tough world.

It was years after his father's death that Bob finally summoned up the courage to ask his mother about her husband. Why had this man been so consumed by fear and anger?

His father had been born in Europe at a time between the two great wars. She told him that, as a young boy, he had watched the family farm being ravaged by soldiers from both sides. The family had little to eat and the military trespassers took much of that. Eventually they even took the farm.

Life for many years was one continuous escape, living in barns, stealing food and other necessities wherever they could. Many days, they found the pain of hunger was almost unbearable. But what could one do? He only knew that he had to survive.

His parents finally succumb to the conditions of extreme poverty and homelessness. Their deaths left Bob's dad alone to face the almost unbearable conditions of life. His determination was the only thing that separated him from joining his parents. Now as a teenager, he could look after himself. Somehow he had to escape from this death defying existence.

Shortly after World War Two was over, he heard some people talking about America, the Land of Freedom. Jobs were plenty and so was land ... maybe he could have a farm just like the one he had known as a small child.

Not many months later, he stood on the docks of New York, a lonely immigrant in a country full of strangers. There was no war here but the fighting raged on in his mind, and his life.

Because there was still so much space in these "Americas," he was able to find a nice little piece of land not far from his landing point. It took many years to build it into a real farm with chickens and cows, as he had to work as a mechanic during the day to stay alive.

By the time Bob and his brothers and sisters were born, the dream had come to reality. The farm was everything he had imagined and he had a wife whom he adored. Unfortunately, the lessons of childhood were not easily forgotten. The terrors of living in abject poverty with absolutely nothing except what he could steal continued to take their toll, stealing any chance of peace.

His father had started drinking to sooth the monster inside him. It helped him for a while, or so he believed. The clouds that escaped from the bottle and settled in his mind hid him from the pain ... and the emotional damage he caused to the people he so loved.

Lashing out at life was all he had ever known, so to protect himself further, his strong hands struck anything that tried to come near. His wife and children all learned that life was not a safe place.

Bob realized the intense and very deep love his mother felt for him that he joyfully returned in kind. He knew that this love was the energy that kept him alive through all the pain of his earlier years and was the driving force in his own quest to find his own path, to grow and to blossom in his own way. He came to understand the vital role his mother played in his life. He realized how she had protected him from his father's wrath and how her softness made being alive possible, and worthwhile.

He came to know that the union of the energies of his mother and father had been brought together to create a unique person known as Bob. Through the understanding and realization of who his parents were, Bob came to realize his own expression. He came to understand why he had hidden himself away so many years before.

By taking the time to explore his life, Bob found the real

path he came to fulfil. He saw the internal strength his father had provided him that kept him going no matter what. He embraced the soft strength of his mother that nurtured him when the going got tough. He felt and knew there was more, so much more to life than the pain he had felt as a child.

Understanding the pain his father knew, Bob learned of his own ability for compassion. Coupled with his mother's ability to see through the mist of illusion, right to the heart of the individual, Bob realized his calling to be a counsellor. Who else could better understand and know the terror and the love on the path of life?

With Sally's encouragement, Bob returned to night school with a fervor that could not be quieted. In record time and at the top of his class, Bob achieved his goal and his apprenticeship in solitude was over, once and forever.

Bob had come to know himself.

Life still offered its challenges, but Bob and Sally innately knew that the lessons contained in each day of their lives revealed a deeper, more permanent understanding of their own light. Life was never difficult because they each knew and respected their own inner strength and that of their partner. Standing back to back, the world could only fall to their aspirations, for they realized there was no strength greater than their own true self and their connection to the universe.

Of all the lessons that have come forward during the writing of this book, for me, it is learning to separate myself from all the "stuff" that goes on in my life. By recognizing who I am as an individual, I can look at anything else that exists as being its own self as well. It doe not matter whether the other "self" is human, animal, an emotion or any other thing, it is not me.

By adopting this perception, I firstly recognize myself as an individual unit and secondly, I keep myself separated from all the other goings-on in life.

This identification allows me to maintain dominion over myself at any time.

What does that mean to me? When I get into a situation with another person where the emotions are flying high, I know that participating in the event does not endanger my existence. I perceive four entities. Let me give you an example.

Bob and Sally are having a discussion about the possibility of having children. Sally really wants to be a mom. Bob is very hesitant, in fact fearful of the idea.

Because Bob and Sally know their own personal blends, the process is easily managed and turned into a growth opportunity. In days of old, this conversation could have turned into a "relationship breaker" (if Bob would have even been in a relationship).

When they realize there is an issue developing, they prepare to discuss it, both taking some time to get themselves relaxed and clear-minded. They remind themselves that there are four entities involved in the conversation. Not one of them is in danger of "losing face." They are: Bob, Sally, Bob's ego and Sally's ego.

By recognizing the importance of each other and their egos, safety becomes a given rather than an issue. As the discussion evolves, there is no competition to win the other over. The discussion centres around two separate issues: What Sally's needs are that she hopes to satisfy through having children, and, what Bob's concerns are regarding why he does not want to have children.

By detaching themselves from the issues, both people are easily able to explore the thoughts and feelings that form the basis that caused the discussion to birth in the first place.

Will Sally and Bob have kids? Who knows? Having kids is only a secondary concern to this particular conversation. The inner learning that evolves from this opportunity, if handled properly, can only bring them closer together. Through that closeness, they will determine their destiny. The main issue for them is getting to the bottom of their perceptions, so that they can develop a more harmonious relationship both with themselves and each other.

Remember, the whole purpose behind "Embracing the Blend" is to give you a basis from which you can anchor your perceptions of the world. This base is uniquely yours that was created from the blending of the beliefs that you developed as you lived your life. By recognizing your uniqueness in the world and embracing it, you offer to life, a unique gift that only you can give.

Every person wants to do his or her part in contributing to the evolution of life. As you Embrace Your Blend, the inner knowledge of your life purpose comes to your consciousness and expresses. What greater satisfaction can there be than living and expressing your "raison d'etre (reason for being)?

For every student on the path of life, it is my heart felt desire that each of you adopt this short message as your personal mantra.

Loving myself is my ultimate goal. Giving myself the space and opportunity to just be me, the only thing I truly can ever be. Loving me enough to separate myself from the perceptions of my ego, so that I can stand free and be the mighty oak that is my true soul expression.

Through recognizing "me" I accept myself for who I truly am. I know that the "stuff" in which I participate in life is separate from me. I know that my body is a vehicle that allows me to function on this planet and my mind and ego help me to perceive and understand the information I interact with.

Knowing my true self keeps me safe. Knowing my true self provides an anchor allowing me to deal with the events of my life without losing myself.

Knowing myself also helps me know that since I am not anything else but me, I am lovable and loved.

Life is an incredible journey, which takes all of our lives to truly embrace, but as a Sufi mystic once said,

"A journey of a thousand miles begins with the first step."

By taking the opportunity to look at yourself fairly, then choosing your best option for that situation, you focus your attention on the best outcome for you at that time. Each decision that is made in this manner helps to forge a stronger character that supports you in living a healthy life style. The gift from this process is wisdom, the greatest gift we can possess and pass on to others.

We are all in this game of life together. None of us get out of it alive, so we need to all work together to share what we have learned.

That way, we all grow, so that the world benefits. Every person and situation we interact with in life needs to be honored and appreciated. By doing so, we create a much larger, more loving energy for all to participate in. The result is more rapid growth for each of us and mankind collectively.

The Bagavagita, a sacred Hindu Sanskrit scripture says,

**"When the student is ready,
the teacher will appear."**

In days of old, the teacher was identified as a single person with greater knowledge than we knew. Today's teacher is every person and situation in our life. There is a lesson in every minute of every day, for you and me and everyone else. All we have to do is be open to sharing and learning.

Too much of the common trend toward living in this present form of life is unconscious. The only way to true happiness and true learning is by consciously choosing the outcome for the moment we are in that we desire. This causes a domino effect that we can manage by focusing on our desired outcome. If we focus on receiving the best possible outcome at any time, we can expect to receive the greatest benefits.

So what would a person expect to find by "Embracing their Blend?"

Although the initial period of the process may be rough, due to resistance by the ego to let go of its control and embrace the new process, a much higher, more profound level of understanding will surround and permeate your life. Difficult situations will still occur, however, your ability to handle these situations will minimize the effect. After all, you know they are no threat to you. Life will become a much easier place to be. Your health will be more balanced and life more satisfying.

Embracing the Blend conveys consciously moving your life forward in a manner that works for you, consistently turning your dreams into the reality that is your innate truth, rather than having to maintain a tactical defense program while trying to thwart off a continuous flow of perceived dangers from others.

Embracing The Blend recognizes ultimately knowing and embracing all the energies that came together to create you, past, present and future so that you can live in the fullness of all that is yours.

The people in our lives will also be affected by our changes. As we shine our light, we automatically provide the medium to allow others to shine theirs as well. Our relationships will be more positive and life enhancing.

Can you imagine what it would be like to live in a world where people truly cared about each other? A world where people consciously chose to do what innately was right, rather than choosing to act out in defense or by committing crimes? Could you imagine a world where our social and political leaders actually supported implementing rules that benefited society's evolution at large, rather than for specialized groups?

We, as individuals, always benefit most when society as a whole benefits.

As we come to know ourselves better, our children will automatically pattern themselves in a healthy way after us and embrace our life skills. They will not have to create defences for their survival; they will be able to really live the life we have only been able to dream about!

Your children will actually be able to use their minds for creating outcomes of true value and social evolution. Maybe, just maybe, life will begin to make sense. Wouldn't that be a dream worth pursuing?

Is knowing yourself important enough to you?

Can you risk leaving behind those old comfortable beliefs and take a chance by exposing your true self? Are you willing to take the risk so you can truly know love?

All you have to do is allow yourself the privilege of knowing and being who you truly are by letting go of the illusion and embracing what feels right. It is a big gamble but if you stay with it, it will pay off like you could never have known.

Well my friend, I truly hope that our conversation has be a valuable adventure for you. Now that you have begun your own conscious journey, please continue the unveiling and most importantly, enjoy. Love the challenging times as much as the good times, then every event will be much easier.

So just like it worked out for Bob and Sally, it's already in you right now, all you have to do is choose to participate in **Embracing the Blend.**

Once you have taken the leap into the formerly "unknowable" parts of yourself, you will notice a sense of exhilaration every time you encounter a situation that used to be looked at as "Oh well, that's just me."

Once you embrace your own power and get to know and enjoy the feeling of "me," you will look forward to the formerly dreaded times because you know you have nothing to fear.

We are designed by our nature to be awesome. All we have to do is take the time to connect with ourselves and let the "awesome" come out.

I wish you all the wonder, success, health and great abundance that is yours already.

A Message From The Author

Photo courtesy of Dee
Lippingwell Photo Studios

From the earliest days of my childhood the supply of questions has never ended, nor the causes of them. Like everyone today, my life has been filled with challenges, some of them easily answered, some almost killed me.

Then one day I woke up to the realization that my life does not have to be a continuum of risking my neck just because my mind was bent on self-destruction. I knew in my heart there had to be a different, better way to live so I set out to find it.

For over 30 years I studied the mystical arts, energetic healing, emotional and core belief work. Being a true observer and participant of life in the trenches taught me what I give to you in this book, tempered by a strong will to live.

What's my motivation to share my observations?

I want you and everyone on this planet earth to find and live in your own strength and individual truth. I believe we all have it; we just need to know it, own it and live it. There is no university that will ever teach you this truth because it is yours already. You just have to accept it. At no other time in the existence of mankind on earth has it been more important for each of us to walk in our own truth, for if we choose not to be true to ourselves, we give our lives over to others who do not care.

Through the words of this book, I present to you a gift that can take you to the very centre of yourself based on the true love you were created in. You will understand how fear and misunderstanding have owned much of your life. From these writings you can extract the tools to assist you to take back your life and live in the freedom of conscious choice.

Beneath all the stories in your head is your true self in all of its splendour and glory waiting for you to come home.

Enjoy! I would love to hear from you. My website is www.powerofsafety.com.

Love & Light

Monty C. Ritchings

Monty Clayton Ritchings is a writer, healing facilitator, lay counsellor, business person, mystic and Dad who resides near Vancouver, BC Canada.

Product Order Form

Name: _____

Address: _____

City: _____Prov/State: _____

Country:_____Postal/Zip Code: _____

Phone: (_____) _____E-mail:_____

Mail orders please send to:
Monty C. Ritchings
9668 148 Street, Suite 107
Surrey, BC   V3R 0W2

For information on booking Monty to speak to your
Organization or to place an order today
Call 604.957.9068   or   E-mail montycritchings@gmail.com

Products

Item	Price
Embracing the Blend - paperback 261 pgs	21.95
Stamp Out Stress	21.95
Free Abundance (coming soon)	
Total Order (Can $):	

Quantity discounts available. Shipping/handling not included.

Charge my _____Visa _____Mastercard

Card Number:_____

Exp Date:_____Name on Card:_____

Signature:_____

Please allow 4—6 weeks for delivery.

Notes